Mr DIGWELL

TRADITIONAL & TRUSTED

A Year in the Garden

An invaluable resource for every gardener from novice to expert

© Haynes Publishing, 2012

The right of Paul Peacock to be identified as the author of this Work has been asserted
by him in accordance with the Copyright, Designs & Patents Act 1988.

All rights reserved. No part of this publication may be reproduced, stored in a retrieval system
or transmitted, in any form or by any means, electronic, mechanical, photocopying, recording
or otherwise, without prior permission in writing from the publisher.

First published in 2012

A catalogue record for this book is available from the British Library

ISBN: 978-0-857331-71-7

Published by Haynes Publishing, Sparkford, Yeovil,
Somerset BA22 7JJ, UK
Tel: 01963 442030 Fax: 01963 440001
Int. tel: +44 1963 442030 Int. fax: +44 1963 440001
E-mail: sales@haynes.co.uk
Website: www.haynes.co.uk

Haynes North America Inc., 861 Lawrence Drive,
Newbury Park, California 91320, USA

Images © Mirrorpix

Creative Director: Kevin Gardner
Designed for Haynes by BrainWave

Printed and bound in the US

TRADITIONAL & TRUSTED

A Year in the Garden

An invaluable resource for every gardener from novice to expert

Featuring a Month by Month Guide
to Easy & Practical Gardening

Paul Peacock

Summer to Autumn

Autumn to Winter

Winter to Spring

January always starts as a catch up. By rights we should have been sowing onion seeds in December and planting shallots on the shortest day of the year. There may not be much major work in the winter, but if you have a little warmth there is a lot to be getting on with in the sowing line.

One of the problems is guilt. People think they should get out there, seeds in hand, and sow to their heart's content – only to find that by the end of February they have a lot of plants that are too leggy to grow properly. So the watchword for winter is patience.

Although the days lengthen in February, they are still cold. This is a good time for covering soil with black plastic, to help warm it. Turning compost will make you sweat on the coldest of days; some of our seeds are now popping through their pots; and the manure that has been brewing all the year is now liberally placed around roses, rhubarb and young fruit.

March comes in like a lion and goes out like a lamb. The whole garden is beginning to change and the greenhouse is full of growing seedlings. The aroma of blackcurrants fills the wind as you prepare the beds, and there is a warm buzz about the garden as leaf buds explode into life.

In this section

January

January in the garden is a confusing month. On one hand the garden languishes along with its wildlife, under a blanket of snow, sleet, rain and wind, but on the other hand there are seeds to be sown, signs of life in borders, fruit needing attention and the ongoing maintenance of paths, greenhouses, water butts and tools. And just sometimes it is nice to sit in the garden shed and watch the garden through the open door, mug of tea in hand.

We are always trying, at this time of the year, to protect plants and bring them on a bit more wherever possible. But you don't need lots of specialist equipment. A cloche warms up during the day, and at night you can keep the frost away by digging a hole and placing a lit night light in it. Central heating for pennies a week.

Another way of cheaply avoiding the frost is to fill plastic lemonade bottles with water and placing them inside a cloche, warming up during the day to give off their heat during the night. A few bricks placed between salad crops does the same job.

Week by week

If it's freezing for the first part of January then the rest of the month is catch up time. If we have snow, go round the garden brushing it off trees; the weight can rip boughs.

The first job of the year is to get your orders in for vegetable and flower seeds. It being winter, you have time to plant bare rooted trees and bushes.

Week 1

Work on compost heaps; turn them over

Lift, divide and replant snowdrops

Protect cordylines, camellias, fuchsias from frost

Sow onions and plant shallots

Week 2

Cover selected beds with black plastic to help warm the soil

Mulch around shrubs and fruit canes and trees with well rotted manure

Disinfect the greenhouse and sharpen tools

Prune buddleia to about 30cm from the ground

Take out any spurious rose growth

Week 3

Prune apples and pears to about two buds on new growth horizontal branches and cut out touching and dead wood

Go round the garden firming in plants with the heel and make sure young trees and shrubs are secure

Spray fruit trees with a copper fungicide to keep them healthy

Dig a runner bean trench if you haven't already and half fill it with well rotted manure

Add lime to beds that will be taking brassicas

Week 4

Sow tomatoes indoors for an early crop

Check your water supply – taps, are they well insulated? Water butts, are they unfrozen?

Smash the ice on garden ponds to allow oxygenation for wildlife and stop the ice breaking the liner

Sow caulis and cabbages – variety 'All Year Round' for an early summer crop

Maintain garden furniture, so you can have a good sit down in summer

TOMATOES

Tomatoes fresh from the vine have just about the most amazing flavour in the world. Tomatoes are easy plants to get going, but high maintenance once they start growing. You can have early tomatoes in the greenhouse or on the windowsill – especially if you use the cherry varieties, though all the others do quite well too. Obviously, these plants are not going outside yet, and will need plenty of warmth until the last frosts are gone.

Use the module system to sow tomatoes, placing two or three seeds into each cell of moist compost. Then all we have to do is discard all but the best growing seedlings and leave one per cell to continue growing. We are not going to prick out and we are not going to touch the plants at all, apart from discarding the ones we don't like.

Finally, grow these in a fairly warm place until they become about 15cm tall. You can then transplant them into 12cm pots of compost. Make a hole in the compost and, holding the plug, push it out with your thumb, so you have the shoots roots enveloped in compost. This "plug" then fits in the hole in the pot and you have no need to actually touch the leaves or stem at all.

Tomatoes that are going out in the garden need to be "hardened off" – that is, keep them outside during May and bring them back inside at night. Those to be grown indoors can be moved to the greenhouse or polytunnel in late April.

Top tips for growing great tomatoes

Support the plants with stakes or string

Remove side shoots – pull off the branches that appear between leaves and stem

Water weekly until the flowers appear, then water every three days, or daily in really hot weather

Feed weekly with tomato feed – the cheap fertilizer is good enough

Pinch out the top of the plant when you have three or five trusses of tomatoes

It's easy!

The key to good tomatoes is water, feed and warmth, and as low humidity as you can manage. Always water evenly – and don't miss a watering opportunity.

There is an amazing variety of tomatoes to grow, and although varieties like 'Moneymaker' and 'Alicante' are old favourites – and perfectly good too – why not splash out on something new. 'Beefmaster F1' is a huge tomato – ideal for sandwiches, and full of flavour.

A blight tolerant variety, 'Fandango F1' is a heavy cropper and full of flavour – and ripens easily. A yellow variety looks great in a salad; 'Golden Sunrise' is considered by many to be the best flavoured tomato you can grow.

How to condition your soil

By far the best time to deal with your soil and to clear your beds, to fertilize them and set them right for next year, is when you take the crops, back in the autumn. The very worst thing you can do is simply leave the beds to the weeds.

Types of soil

Soils are graded according to the size of the particles that make them up. This sounds quite scientific, but in reality it is fairly commonsense, and it gives you an insight into how to deal with them. Also, the way the particles react with water is important too, because water has some amazing forces with it, without which the garden wouldn't work at all.

Sandy soil

This soil is predominantly made up of large (in soil terms) particles. Around 1mm in diameter, these are too big for the water to hold together and it just pours through. Sandy soils are therefore very dry, well-drained soils.

If your soil is predominantly sandy, it will need a lot of watering in the summer and during dry spells. You can improve the amount of water held in the soil by adding compost, freshly rotted down and full of nutrients.

Another problem with sandy soil is it's low in nutrients because it's constantly washed clean by the water. Again, using compost slows this process. If you add compost each year, you will get good soil within five or six years.

Loam

This soil contains some sand, but the majority of it has particles 10 times smaller. Water holds them together, and yet there are enough air spaces to allow oxygen to get to the roots. This is generally the soil we are all looking to grow in, but there can be some drawbacks.

In loam, water moves easily from one part of the garden to another, and in wet months this soil can be waterlogged. If so, you need to improve the drainage – which can be anything from adding a little sand or grit, or even digging a channel.

Maintain fertility by adding compost or organic fertilizer, and keep an eye on how well plants grow in it over the years.

Another thing to look at is the colour. If it starts to lighten and dry out in droughts, add organic matter – to keep it dark and moist.

Living soil

A good soil is a living thing, a community of all kinds of organisms. When I started gardening we used to think the best thing to do was to take away all the "bad" animals, leaving what we thought were only beneficial organisms. Now we know differently – though our gardens were pretty good, we no longer treat soil to remove bugs, save perhaps chafer grubs and the ever-present slugs and snails.

Clay soils

Clay has little or no oxygen in it because the air spaces are filled with water. The force of the water drives all the air out. The other problem is that clay is usually cold and this will set your plants back a few weeks.

Increasing the aeration of clay is not particularly simple, but with effort you can make clay into a half decent soil. Dig into it as much as you can and add lime to the clay, which will help break it up and also helps make some of the tiny clay particles stick together to make a more crumbly structure.

Then add, in equal volumes, sand and compost, and try to mix in as much as you can. Continuing this, year after year, will start to build a half decent soil – and remember, where there is clay, there is also water, so eventually you will have a good, life-giving soil.

Water

Without water, even the richest soils are barren. The way to improve the amount of water available in the soil is to add organic matter. This can be anything from farmyard manure or spent hops to garden compost. Ideally, this organic matter is dug into the soil in the autumn and acts like a sponge, retaining water. You can add some now, in February, however – so long as it is really well rotted.

If you squeeze a ball of soil and it drips water, it is far too wet!

I used to get away with putting a few trays of soil in the oven and baking them whenever I needed some sterilized soil. However, that came to an end when I baked compost and it set on fire. The easiest way is to steam the soil outside, in a drum.

You need to sterilize compost and soil from time to time if you are going to grow some seedlings that are very susceptible to "damping off".

How to make compost

There are so many new ways of composting out there, such as worm compositors and special bacterial digesters, and all kinds of other clever ways. I still think the simple way is the best one, and by using my system you can easily have good compost in six months.

To my mind, compost has to be hot compost. Only by getting the material hot will you kill weed seeds and compost-borne diseases. It's obvious really: when something rots, it is full of decaying bacteria, and this has to be killed by heat if you are not going to bring these decaying organisms into the garden.

Making good quality compost, for me, starts in the winter, when you dig a hole in the ground about 30cm deep and about a metre square. This is lined with straw and a liberal amount of garden waste is then placed on top. This provides the foundation for the heap, which is built upon with waste until it is about six inches proud of the hole.

At this stage cover the growing mound with tarpaulin or plastic or old carpet: anything to keep the rain off and the heat in. Alternatively you can build a frame around the heap – my favourite frame is made from old pallets, but be careful as these can be quite heavy.

Activators

You can buy compost starters or make them. A shovel full of chicken manure, a few inches of compost from another heap, a mixture of soil, straw and a bucket of urine – all these will do the trick.

Build up the heap by adding about six inches of material at a time. You will have to collect the waste in a bucket and add it all at once – this way the heap does not lose heat every time you have something to compost.

After every six inches of rotting material, you need to then put a few centimetres of soil on the top, so as to make a layer cake of soil and rotting material, until the heap reaches about a metre high. In effect you are layering rotting material with soil.

Grass

If you must add grass, put it between some newspaper to soak up the excess liquid. While we're on the subject of liquid, every now and again pour some water onto the heap – all living things need a drink now and again.

Mr **DIGWELL**

What not to compost

Wood and twigs

Bread

Meat

Fish

Gravy

Turn it over

After between three to six months, depending on the weather (if it is hot, nearer to three months; cold, nearer to six months) the heap needs turning over. This is to aerate the compost and speed its completion.

How do you know it is ready?

The compost is crumbly, sweet-smelling and uniform. It will have a light texture, and when squeezed will stick together in a ball but fall apart very easily.

The best use of compost is to grow young plants. I make a great seed compost with 50% home-made compost, 25% soil and 25% sand, mixed and shaken through a riddle.

Keep the heap warm and you will have great compost!

POTATOES

How to grow potatoes

Gone are the days when we grew a plot full of potatoes. But new potatoes and potatoes for Christmas are as popular as ever.

The thing about potatoes is they are very versatile, so long as you keep them frost free. If you can grow them indoors, they can be started off at almost any time of the year. Within a week of the potatoes pushing themselves out of the soil gardeners are earthing them up to be sure the tubers are not exposed to light and turn green. This is a job for a draw hoe, but I have seen a number of gardeners do it quite differently.

Should I chit my potatoes?

Chitting is the process the potato does for itself. It is simply the action of an enzyme on the buds of the tuber, making them grow. Seed potatoes are normally bought in the late winter and then left in trays, out of the frost. Over the next couple of months the eyes (buds on the surface of the potato) start to grow, and then small thin stems grow from the potato.

I asked a chap why he had huge prism-shaped mounds across his plot, geometrically perfect and about 1.5 metres wide at the bottom and 50cm at the tip, which was about 75cm above the soil bed. He said it was the way they did it in Ireland – the potatoes are plunged into the centre, as then the growers are certain that the new tubers will never see daylight. The interesting thing is he grew everything in these mounds, carrots, cabbages, leeks – the lot.

Problems with potatoes are rare but devastating. I say rare but blight is becoming more prevalent. There are two types of blight, early and late, and you can spray to prevent them – but on the whole it is best to keep humidity to a minimum, something that is not always easy. Blight is at its worst in late summer when there has been a drought followed by warm rain. The spores are very active – if you see a browning and blackening of leaves, whip the shawl off quick and then burn them. Then dig up the potatoes and wash them under the allotment tap. With luck you will have caught the tubers before they are rotted.

Remember, of course, that you can take the infection into the greenhouse and infect the tomatoes. Always wash and change your clothes before you go into the greenhouse.

February

How long does the winter last! I always brace myself for a hard time of it in the garden during February; you can get every type of weather in a single day, and there seems to be little sun around to warm the soil. And, in this month, you also find the greatest variation from one end of the country to the other.

In the balmy south you are beginning to see the garden wake up, while in the frozen north it is still fast asleep. But you can take heart, as by the end of the month gardens everywhere will be bursting into life.

Fighting the elements

February brings a lot of moisture to the garden, and you need to counter its effect on your plants. First of all keep a note of where the puddles are forming – maybe this needs remedial drainage when the soil is easier to work on. Secondly, make sure all your plants – particularly the shrubs – are very secure as it can get quite windy.

Working in the greenhouse

Bad weather makes the greenhouse very cosy. Take the time to clean it, and disinfect all your tools, pots and various other implements. Clean up your beds and so on. And yes! It is time to wake some of your plants, such as dahlias, and place them in warm pots of compost – not peat!

Week by week

February can be a nervous month. If it's mild then you are always worrying about when the frosts will come or, even worse, if it's likely to be a freezing March. But then your garden can be completely covered in snow throughout February, and you are confined to the greenhouse.

The first job of the month is maintenance – sharpen and clean your tools and get some reading up done while there is still time.

Week 1

Add grease bands to fruit trees to deter climbing insects

Finally finish the job (if it's not snowy) of clearing the last of the fallen leaves

Check your pots for spring sowing and replace as necessary

Make sure your insulation in the greenhouse is still in place and fill your heaters

Week 2

Make sure your raspberries and other cane fruit are pruned appropriately.

You can continue to plant bare-rooted trees – if the ground isn't too hard

Turn the compost over and prepare a place for manure deliveries

Week 3

Check your paths for cracks and remove moss

If you haven't already, mulch your one-year-old trees as well as any fruit, like rhubarb

Tidy beds and cover remaining ones with black plastic to warm them for early planting

Week 4

Make sure bird feeders are full

Break any ice on ponds

Sow early tomatoes and peppers

Check on hardwood cuttings for signs of growth

Greenhouses and polytunnels

The greenhouse and polytunnel need a little TLC at this time of the year – cleaning and making sure everything is ready for the spring. Freezing weather plays havoc with greenhouses but a little work cures all ills.

Removing algae from the greenhouse and the polytunnel is really important since the more algae, the darker the inside.

Draughts that invade the greenhouse – through the door or a broken pane of glass – cool the area so much that even greenhouse heating will not protect the plants.

Try to remove all the moss growing between the panes of glass as when the frost comes wet moss expands and cracks the glass.

Make sure you insulate the greenhouse well, and that you check it regularly each day. I use bubble wrap, which is quite cheap these days, and tape it to various points in the greenhouse. I don't cover the roof because I like to get as much unhindered light into the greenhouse as I can.

Insulate the polytunnel too, but given that they are much bigger than greenhouses, you can create a room, by making a wall of bubblewrap, that you keep warm, leaving the rest of the tunnel cool.

I keep a water butt *inside* the greenhouse, which warms up during the day and releases its warmth at night. Another tip is to put a candle in the greenhouse. Place the candle inside a hollow concrete block to make a cheap but effective heater.

Sometimes you will need a specific temperature to allow seeds to germinate and for this you can use a propagator. It will require a power supply in your greenhouse but the rest of the greenhouse can be kept at cooler temperatures for overwintering plants, such as potted camellias.

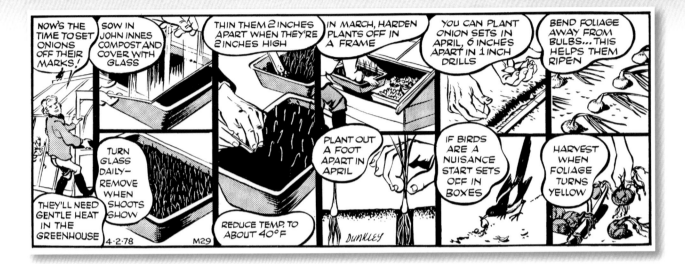

It's traditional to sow onions on Boxing Day, but there is always too much to do then! However, sow the onions just afterwards, in trays of compost, with a little sand added, and keep them at around 12°C. This way you will have plants ready for transplanting in March or April. Thin them out and don't overwater them because they can rot.

It is not feasible to recreate high summer in the winter greenhouse. You only end up with increased disease. This is because the majority of plants know it is winter because of the length of the day rather than how warm it is, so trying to grow summer plants, or even start summer bedding in the winter is heading for trouble.

The very best use of the greenhouse or polytunnel is to extend the growing season by providing a month or more at the beginning of the year and a similar amount at the end. So you can start seeds in February where outside they would only germinate in April or May.

In the shelter and warmth of the greenhouse, you can create "perfect" plants because they are not bashed around by wind and rain, and there is often less chance of insect pests nibbling at them.

Growing more exotic plants like melons is the ideal use for the polytunnel. I have to say that in the summer, when the melons are ripe and sweet, the tunnel smells wonderful. The amount of space you need to grow melons can make it a little hit and miss, and mostly, if I transplant them outside, they are something of a disappointment when the summer is poor. In the tunnel, though, they are always perfect!

Try to keep the warmest part of your greenhouse or polytunnel as near to 7°C as you can!

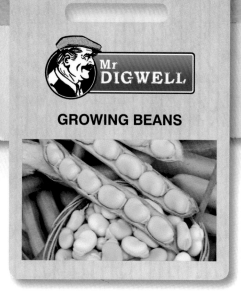

GROWING BEANS

Broad, runner, French and other beans

Beans are much more than a staple, they're tasty too! Relatively easy to grow, you can eat them raw, salted, cooked or, my favourite way – home-made baked beans!

Broad beans

You need well-drained soil that will retain a little water but not too much. Cold water chills the seedlings so they grow very slowly. Having said that, bean seeds of all types prefer cool conditions for germination.

The soil needs a little preparation: adding some well rotted manure is ample, but when? Some people add manure to the soil before sowing, but I tend to wait until spring because I don't want to encourage too much shoot growth at this early time of year.

Broad beans are grown in double rows. That is, each row is made up of two lines of seeds, planted 15cm apart. The next double row is 75cm away from the first.

Runner beans

Runner beans can either be sown directly into the ground, or started off in 8cm pots, which is the way I prefer. They too like very fertile soil and a lot of support, which is why they are often grown against a trellis of canes or a wigwam – but that wastes a lot of soil.

Giving them a good start in the warm gives better plants, and allows a little leeway in the garden to prepare your spot.

The key to success with runner beans is threefold. Water, gallons of it, is really important. If they dry out, they get tough, small and stringy. Water every day and they will be succulent. Secondly, feed them at least – and I mean at least – every week. A good organic fertilizer is fine. Finally, they need sunshine – keep them in full sun and they will flower readily. In shade all you will get are leaves.

Pick the beans when they are about 25cm long, the more you take, the more flowers will appear to replace them.

French beans

These are easy to grow, low maintenance and very productive. Give them plenty of manure and the beans will taste all the sweeter. These are sown in May or June, in very rich soils, and they harvest from August onwards. They need to be kept weed free and well watered. As with runner beans, pick them freely and often.

Bedding plants and gloxinias

The summer might seem to be a lifetime away, and it might be freezing outside, but it is time to think about summer bedding.

There are two schools regarding summer bedding, the "old school", as I am frequently called, favour floral displays of themed colourful beds. Newer trends in gardening include interplanting all kinds of plants with a companion. This latter style of plantsmanship works whether you are planting bedding flowers amongst vegetables that you will eat or growing floral and architectural plants for display.

Making a floral display in a flower bed might be out of fashion, but it is great fun. You can design your beds and create super effects, blending colours, textures and forms.

QUICK TIP: *Have plants that go from tall at the back to short at the front. To increase the appearance of depth, have light-coloured tall plants with dark-coloured short plants at their feet.*

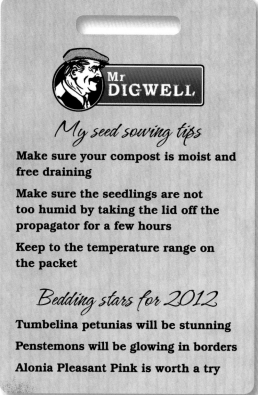

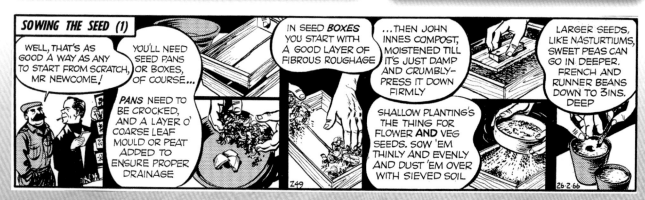

Crop rotation

Crop rotation used to maintain soil fertility, but in modern gardens it is more to do with pest control.

In many cases freedom from pests is considerably helped by never growing the same crop in consecutive years in the same piece of soil. So you rotate your crops around the plot.

It doesn't matter how many rotations you set up in the garden – and indeed you might have two different kinds of rotation on the same plot. For example, you might have a root crop, salad and sweetcorn rotation on one part of the plot and a potato, beans, root crop and salad crop rotation on another part of the plot.

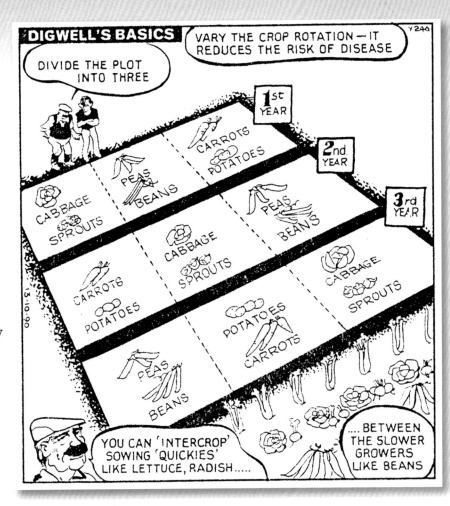

Sometimes pests, like clubroot, can lie dormant for many years, and sometimes the same pest will like to eat more than one crop. But a rotation is useful as a general way in which we can work with nature to keep our gardens healthy.

What about clubroot?

The only surefire way of keeping it at bay is to stop walking on the soil. You transfer the spores on your boots, and

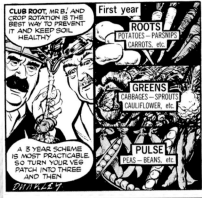

it can take a decade before clubroot dies out. You can help your brassicas along by adding lots of lime – really a lot. This way the roots are able to produce a decent plant before they come in contact with the fungus.

Cane and soft fruit

Preparing, mulching and pruning cane and soft fruit are jobs to be getting on with at this time of the year. Confusingly there are two types of fruit: top fruit and soft fruit. I say confusing because, with a few exceptions, all fruit is soft.

Raspberries

Raspberries come in two forms, summer fruiting and autumn fruiting.

Summer fruiting raspberries set fruit on last year's canes, so once they have been harvested, cut them out. Autumn fruiting plants set fruit on this year's growth, so again, cut them out once they have fruited, and new canes will grow next year.

Good old varieties: 'Glen Ample' for summer fruiting types and 'Autumn Bliss' for autumn fruiting.

Blackberries

Such a wonderful plant, blackberries fruit on last year's canes, so again, cut them out once they have been harvested. Usually these plants are grown on a wire fence, where the fruiting canes are tied in. Once the old canes have been cut out, burn them, and tie in the remaining canes for next year's fruiting.

Figs

Ever since I was young I struggled to grow a fig. The variety hasn't changed at all, and we still grow 'Brown Turkey', which nowadays sounds like a medical procedure. It is a self-fertile variety that will develop fruit if kept warm. Eventually I worked out that if you grew it in a pot you could bring it indoors during the very coldest weather. To ensure fruit, grow it in a greenhouse.

Peaches

You will always look like an expert gardener if you grow peaches. I have found that if you travel south from about Derby, you will increasingly get good results against a wall. But north of Derby you need more protection for excellent results.

Pruning looks complex, but it isn't really – just prune to three shoots, which will flower next year.

Cover peaches with a plastic sheet in winter to help reduce peach leaf curl – a fungal infection.

CUCUMBERS

February is the start of a love affair – caring for my cucumbers. To be honest, up here in Lancashire, I have only had real success with those grown under glass, but I have friends "down south" who grow them outside, using old pallets as frames, and jolly nice cucumbers they are too!

Cucumbers like a lot of nutrients and a lot of water and, of course, warmth. There are many varieties, some pimply and spiny, some smooth. Personally, I think

the spiny ones are more flavoursome, but that's a matter of taste. What I can say is the ones you grow at home are so much better than the ones you buy.

In essence you can treat cucumbers a little like tomatoes, in that the key to success is largely the same – feed, water and warmth.

You get male and female flowers; you can tell the females by the ovary behind the petals. These days I try to restrict the cucumbers to about eight per plant by pinching out those I don't want. They will grow happily from a growbag and if you stand a wooden palette at a 45-degree angle you can train the vine over the back, allowing the fruit to rest easily and evenly on the sloping side.

If you live in the south, grow them facing the sun, against a wall.

Winter rose care

One year the frost killed all the new growth on my roses. It was so mild in January that they all grew out and a very sharp frost nipped them all so drastically, I lost them. Don't take any chances in winter – cut back the tender wood!

It's important to remember that at best roses are only half hardy – and new growth is delicate. In the winter, if the weather is mild, they grow readily, and can be easily frostbitten, so I tend to prune them hard. There are plenty of buds to grow out of new wood in the spring.

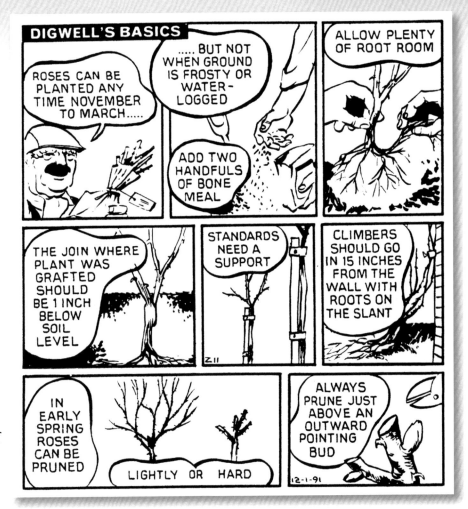

If you cut towards an outwards facing bud, it will grow out and not cross any other branches. You are looking to create a goblet shape where the wind can circulate easily and freely. Branches that touch can damage each other and should be avoided.

When pruning, find a bud that slopes away from the centre of the plant, and cut. When cutting, think about the rain – make a cut so the rain, should it fall on the surface, will fall away from the bud without wetting it.

You can cover the cut surface with some wound paint or a few drops of candle or sealing wax.

Regardless of the type of rose, climbing or standard, the procedure is exactly the same.

Designing a small garden

Gone are the days when formality in design was all-important. You can, if you think carefully about it, create a garden that makes your small space seem larger, longer, wider or just plain old beautiful.

Paved with containers

There is nothing wrong with containers, and nothing wrong with paving either! If you can afford really good paving slabs, the colour and texture will form a backdrop for your planting. If you plant on slate, for example, you might want to grow purples such as agapanthus and alliums.

If you cannot afford good quality paving go for shingle or stones, which have the added benefit that no one is able to walk on it without making a noise – thus deterring unwanted visitors. If, however, you do go for paving, have it professionally laid as this makes all the difference.

> You can fill a small garden easily – and take elements from all the gardens you like.

Teardrop

If you create a path on one side as a teardrop shape, and continue the theme on the other side with planting, you will have a shape to the garden that tricks the mind into thinking there is more to it than there really is. This is because there are many other shapes implicit in the teardrop design – mostly at the corners. Also, the path itself creates the illusion of depth, and the lack of defined symmetry in the shape is a very interesting feature.

The only problem with this design is what goes in the middle. Grass is difficult to cut, stones can work, but containers in the teardrop can spoil the effect. A teardrop-shaped pond at the end, however, accentuates the garden – this makes an ideal small wildlife garden.

Raised beds

It is possible to build raised beds that are a  different shape to the ordinary rectangular ones, thus providing a design feature themselves. Raised beds pick out the horizontal, which makes a small space seem wider and gives you something to walk round. You get to see the beds from all angles, and you can put other containers in the spaces. This can become a clean, modern space, allowing either a contrast between the beds or a subtle development.

Small self-sufficiency garden

The final garden, on the right-hand side of the image opposite, is a good design for a small self-sufficient garden. At the end is a hen hut, one of those all but round ones with a built-in run. Another zigzag path ends in various beds of different shapes, which take up all the available space, and a small circular potager. The circle is the best use of space as long as you can make good use of the areas left over.

In true self-sufficiency tradition you can fit in various hanging baskets and wall-mounted planters for extra growing space while the manure from the hens (and there is usually a lot of it) will feed the garden! A lot of space needs to be given over to hens, and I would suggest that you pave a small garden so they do not mess the soil and you can clean the area more efficiently.

March

In like a lion, out like a lamb. That's the best way to describe March as, although we get mild days there is always a chance of heavy frost and a covering of snow – so be careful not to get carried away and plant your delicates in the cold.

There is much to do in March, but don't panic if you are not able to get all your sowing completed on time – there is always April!

Sowing

Chinese gooseberries are now known as kiwi fruit, but I suppose neither name really fits the bill. They grow to be huge plants, and the variety to get in the UK is 'Jenny'.

QUICK TIP: *Make sure your seedlings get enough water to grow, but too much will make them rot – a disease called "damping off". The best way to beat the carrot fly is to use horticultural fleece.*

Ground preparation

So long as the weather allows, get outside and prepare the ground for all kinds of crops. Onions, carrots, turnips and potatoes all need soil to be fertilized, aerated and crumbly, and warm. Place a sheet of black plastic over the soil for a fortnight to warm it.

It is time to plant the first early potatoes, if you want to eat them in June. Be sure to use soil that has plenty of well rotted manure in it.

Plan an asparagus bed

Now's the time to plant asparagus in a well-prepared bed, and boy does it grow well if it is well protected and warm. This bed will keep you in springtime vegetables for 10 years or more, so it is a good idea to treat it right in the early stages. Lots of manure and – we don't often hear this – work in a couple of spades of sand per plant.

Week by week

March is the time when our plans and preparation start to come together. There is lots of sowing to do, groundwork on the beds in the garden and planting out – and even though everything is growing be careful that the last dregs of winter don't catch you out.

Plants sown in the open need to be protected with a cloche from the cold – and watch out for the wind too as it will buffet your young plants about.

Week 1

Prune apples

You can force rhubarb in a pot

Prune roses – especially to avoid frost

Manure flower beds

Week 2

Sow bedding plants

Give the lawn a good spiking to improve aeration

Plant first early potatoes

Weed strawberries

Week 3

Start sweetcorn indoors

Prepare soil for all crops – make a fine tilth, especially for carrots

Check outdoor water supplies and irrigation systems

Trim hedges before birds are nesting

Week 4

Clean out the pond if warm

Edge the lawn

Last chance to plant bare-rooted trees and bushes

DAHLIAS

Growing dahlias

We dug up our Dahlia tubers and divided them, before covering the cut surfaces with sulphur powder, in the autumn. Having wrapped them in newspaper and kept them frost free, they are now ready for their cycle to begin all over again.

Now it is time to give them a check. Take them from the paper and discard any rotting tubers. They rot for all kinds of reasons: too cold, too rough handling, nibbling mice and hideaway slugs.

The reason for looking at them now is that, as the days grow warmer, any rotting tubers will spoil the whole bunch. Take a good peek, and pot them in compost. They should be going in the ground in May, just a couple of centimetres below the soil surface. Small tubers can be placed in 15cm pots and kept in the greenhouse until July, when they can safely be placed outside.

The other thing about dahlias is that the first shoots they send out can be cut off. Then remove a couple of leaves and pot into new potting compost. I have found that rooting powder isn't necessary – but the fungicide it contains does stop any rot.

These days people are growing dahlias in the border as bedding plants, and moving them on to a different growing position in the following year.

Garden pond

This month do some work on your pond, or begin building one from scratch. It will help a garden come to life as it will be a haven for all kinds of wildlife.

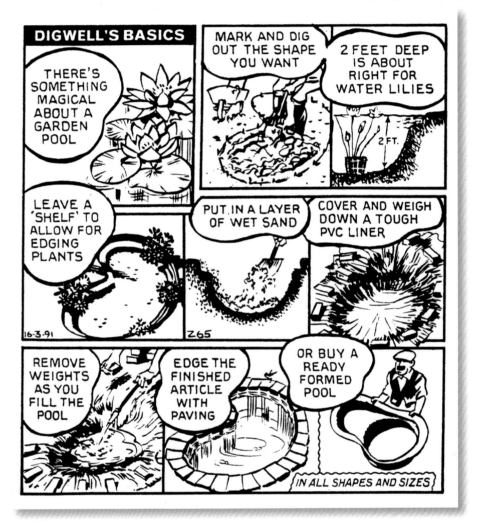

You should site a pond anywhere but the lowest part of the garden. It is fine to put the peripheries of the pond at the wettest and lowest point, especially if you want a very large wetland area. But the body of your pond should always be at a higher point in your garden.

Dig your pond to include some shallow water, a beached area and various levels of depth, going down to at least 60cm.

Once dug out you will need to line the pond so that the rubber sheet does not lie on anything sharp. The weight of water on the plastic will force a stone to pierce it from underneath, and therefore you'll have a leaky pond in a comparatively short time. A 5cm layer of sand will keep the lining in good order. You can also buy pond liner underlay over which you lay your butyl or other waterproof liner.

When you buy your pond liner sheet, you need to take into account the extra surface area of the hole that gives your pond depth.

GREENHOUSE MELONS

Best melons

Melons are the perfect summer fruit and in many parts of the country the growing of them is not as difficult as you would imagine. Once I learned to grow them in ring culture pots (bottomless 30cm pots) I never had problems with them, it is such an easy technique.

People complain of melons not getting anywhere, or only producing male flowers or very small fruits. You can also expect lots of plant growth and little or no flowers. In many ways, the UK is at the limit of the northern range for growing melons. The way to avoid disappointment is feed, water and warmth.

It is sensible, if planning to grow them outside, to transplant the melon plantlet and then cover it with a cloche, keeping it in place until the weather is really warm.

You can tell the difference between male and female flowers. The females have little ovaries behind the petals and the males do not. You can use male flowers to pollinate the females by cutting them off and touching the female parts with the anthers. Once the plants are growing melons, the flowers will diminish. Pull off the petals to avoid blossom end rot and feed the plants weekly.

You need to water daily where possible, a little like tomatoes. The fruits become fuller as they grow and they may need protecting – often in nets attached to a framework or trellis.

These days there are more varieties of melon available that require a shorter growing period. This is perfect as it takes full advantage of our shorter British summers. 'Alvaro' and 'Magenta' are F1 hybrids that do well here – you can expect from four to six fruits.

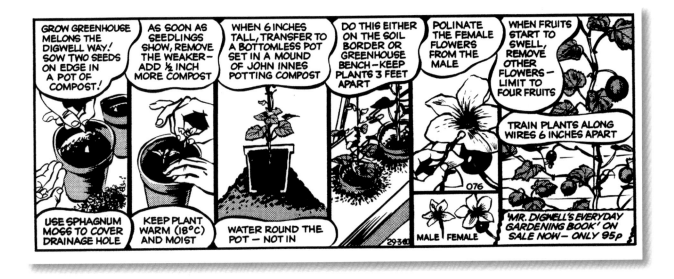

If you are going to grow melons outside, try them against a south facing wall. You get best results from London southwards, though I have seen some good results as far north as Manchester. You are best to keep a plastic sheet over them as much as possible, and sow them indoors, only taking them outside in June – which means growing them in pots until then.

Originating in tropical countries, mostly from South America, melons are not suited to cool climates with predominantly cold driving rain. Draughts and cold rain stunt their growth and promote fungal diseases.

Finally, even though it is June, you still have to harden the plants off for a week – taking them inside during the night and back outside during the day.

CARROTS

Carrots are a wonderful crop for every gardener. While they are relatively easy to grow there are a number of things to think about. I have grown them in many ways over the years and it's easy to cater to their fundamental needs – reasonably free-draining soil with not too many nutrients.

The easiest way to grow carrots is to hoe the soil as much as possible to make a fine tilth – a soil that is crumbly and without lumps. Use a garden line and then scrape a small straight furrow, about a finger's depth, in the soil. You can then sow your seed thinly before covering with soil and watering them in.

You can also fill a large wooden box (or a growbag, a shopping bag or any other receptacle) with a mixture of 50:50 compost and sand, broadcast carrot seeds into it and, without thinning, water and leave them to grow. Within a month of sowing you will have baby carrots, and these will get larger as you randomly take some for the kitchen.

There are so many varieties of carrots that they range from black to yellow in colour, but they are more or less equally easy to grow. There are a number of basic carrot types, of which we tend to grow the 'Nantes' (like a Cuban cigar), the 'Chantenay' (has a definite shoulder and is more carrot shaped), and the 'Imperator' (like a long Roman candle) more than any others.

What we used to call maincrop carrots are sown in May and June and thinned out in June and July, giving you full-sized carrots in August. Maintain regular watering, and don't let them suffer periods of drought followed by periods of overwatering to compensate – the roots will swell and split.

The spacing of plants

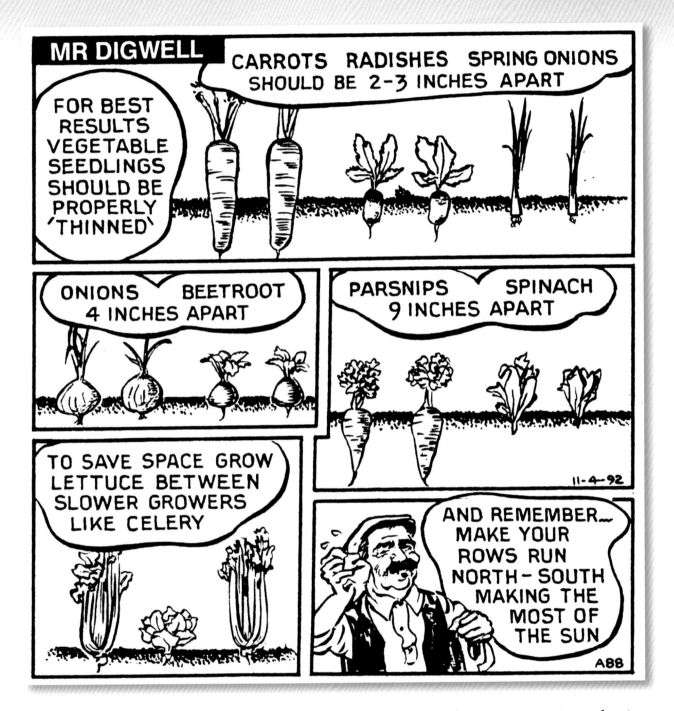

The correct spacing of plants allows your vegetables to grow to their optimum size and not become stunted. What seems like wasted space when the plant is small, will soon be used by vigorously growing, healthy, plants.

Also, spacing allows the plants to grow into the available space. What seems like a waste of space when the plant is small is quickly filled in as growth continues.

QUICK TIP: *You can fill in the space between some plants with salads and smaller plants – get the most out of your soil.*

LEEKS

Leeks are fun plants to sow and grow. You have a lot of latitude with them, and you can generally produce a good crop in most soils. We eat a lot of leeks, and I sow them liberally in a large container and leave them to grow – watering freely and feeding sparingly until it is time to transplant.

Use a bulb planter to pull out a plug of soil, into which you will simply drop a leek plantlet. Having "planted" your leek simply fill the hole with water.

Plant leeks about 60cm apart. Once they start growing and the weather starts drawing soil into the holes, you will see the leeks bedding into the space.

Some people draw soil up around the developing trunks – to give white length up the leek – some (including myself these days) don't bother. Varieties like 'Musselburgh' and 'Neptune' do not need any earthing up as they are self-blanching. Myself, I quite like a bit of green stem and I often grow 'Carlton', an F1 variety, because it has really good germination and grows well in the cold.

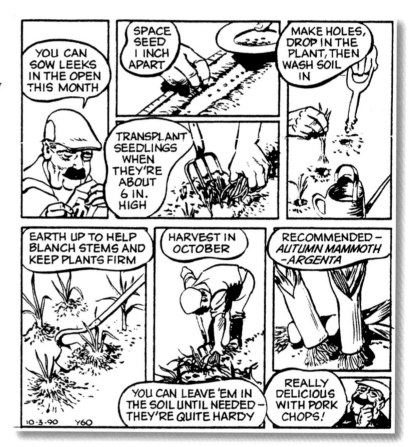

In preparation for the winter, heel in your leeks so they don't rock in the wind, and cover them with fleece to protect them from the rain.

In the winter it is not a bad idea to cover your leeks with horticultural mesh to save them from the worst of the weather.

Using peat

On some of my older cartoons you will see me advocating the use of peat. These days, with peat bogs fast disappearing, we do not use it in our gardens for environmental reasons.

We've learned that there are far better alternatives to peat, leaf mould is particularly good. Its only drawback is it takes a while to prepare – 12 months in fact – but it's well worth it. It is a free resource and whereas it is difficult to call it organic – especially in towns – it is completely natural.

Where I live there are hundreds of trees, the paths and roads are full of them. So I sweep the leaves up to compost them myself. They are best composted in a cage of chicken wire, but even that isn't necessary. I often just make a huge pile at the bottom of the garden and in 12 months the leaf mould has become a perfect peat-like compost.

Leaf mould is quite different to common garden compost because it is largely made up of a single material, and therefore has a basic structure. It is fine grained and fairly rich in nutrients. It is also very good at soaking up moisture, just like peat, and if you let it dry it is easily mulched around the garden without getting messy.

You can make leaf mould in a compost bin if you like, but you have to water it often – say once a month. You can also make it in sacking or string bags that allow the air to circulate, speeding the rotting process.

Before you pile the leaves prior to composting, sweep them together into little hills and allow any wildlife to escape. This only takes a day or so, but is well worth it. Your big pile will become home to hedgehogs if you are lucky and if you are not badgers will play in them, throwing the leaves all over the place.

Mr DIGWELL

STRAWBERRIES

Succulent strawberries

Strawberries, so named because they are grown on straw to keep them off the mud, are perhaps one of the most wonderful fruits in the garden. They take a year to get into full production, then have two stunning years before succumbing to viral diseases. But don't worry – they grow their own replacements.

IT'S TIME FOR PERPETUAL STRAWBERRIES – THEY CROP AND CROP AGAIN FROM AUGUST ONWARDS

WORK IN PEAT, PLANT 18 IN. APART IN ROWS 2 FT. APART

GIVE PLANTS REGULAR FEEDS – IN DRY SPELLS A MULCH OF COMPOST

M70

WHEN BERRIES FORM, PROTECT THEM WITH PLASTIC SHEET

USE CAPTAN TO GUARD AGAINST GREEN MOULD

PLANTS LAST ABOUT 3 YEARS, SO, IN LATE SUMMER, PEG DOWN AND ROOT RUNNERS TO REPLACE OLD STOCK

GENTO IS A GOOD VARIETY

TO ENSURE A GOOD CROP REMOVE FIRST FLOWERS

OR STRAW OR PLASTIC RUFFS

AND NET AGAINST BIRDS

DUNKLEY

25·3·78

NOW'S THE TIME TOO TO SOW ALPINE STRAWBERRIES. THEY'RE DELICIOUS AND FINE AS GROUND COVER PLANTS

Strawberries can be planted any time between October and March, and are possibly best if overwintered. They are tough little plants – if a little greedy for nutrients. How you protect them from the soil, and indeed from slugs and snails, is up to you, but for me straw is still as good as anything. From February onwards, if you cover them with a cloche they will start to flower quickly, and you will have a crop by the end of May.

MR DIGWELL

STRAWBERRY PLANTS SHOULD HAVE FORMED RUNNERS BY NOW...

...SO THIS IS THE TIME TO CASH IN ON A STOCK INCREASE!

SINK IN A 3 IN. POT FILLED WITH SOIL

PIN DOWN THE RUNNER WITH A PIECE OF WIRE

B158

IN 4 TO 5 WEEKS, ROOTS WILL HAVE FORMED

AND STEMS CAN BE CUT

REMOVE NEW PLANTS FROM THEIR POTS

THEN PUT OUT, KEEPING THE CROWN FREE FROM SOIL

3-7-93

These plants send out stems that cling to the ground, called runners. Along the length of the runners you will find a leaflet, which will grow into a new plant. Take some compost in a pot and place the plantlet on top – anchoring it with a "U" nail or a pebble. This plantlet will grow into a new plant, genetically identical to its parent.

Once the runner starts to wither, cut it off and put the plant in the sun. You can overwinter these pots in a cool greenhouse, ready for planting next year. Brand new plants bought from the nursery are best planted in October.

Strawberries take a year to get going, only moderately fruiting in the first summer. If fed well, this plant will be prolific for two years.

They suffer from greenfly attack – and the greenflies bring with them all kinds of viral infections too. You will notice, after the third year, the yield falling and the plant looking somewhat scruffy. Consequently it is best to grow strawberries in separate small beds, representing first to third-year plants. Replace them in their fourth year – that is, you will replace around one-third of your total stock.

Strawberries grow well in all kinds of containers from hanging baskets to pots. It might be hard to get a barrel these days, but one of the best ways to grow strawberries I have seen is in a container on legs, a bit like those 1960s planters you used to see in living rooms. The fruit hangs over the side of the container and is unmolested by snail or soil.

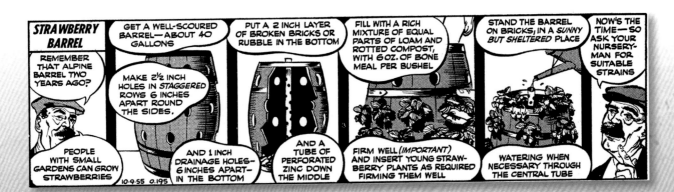

ASPARAGUS

Growing asparagus

The important thing for growing asparagus is sandy soil. Also getting the plant to grow enough so as to keep that fine balance between productivity and plant health. Take too many spears early in the life of the plant and you weaken it so it dies off. All in all growing asparagus is a balancing act.

It's becoming increasingly popular as asparagus looks really impressive in the garden – with its translucent mist of fronds – but best of all it's really tasty on the plate.

Dig a trench with a mound in the centre over which you spread the roots of the asparagus crowns. Fill in the trench with a mixture of 50% compost, 20% soil, 20% sand and 10% good quality fertilizer. Way back we used to use bonemeal, and you can still get it, but you are advised to wear gloves when handling it.

Plant the crowns in April or May, and when they grow cover them with soil, using a draw hoe just like potatoes. This is to give the plant some support, and keep the crown nice and warm. In their first summer, give the plants a good feed of organic fertilizer to give them a great boost.

In the autumn, a lot of people worry about asparagus – what to do with the fronds. Should they be left to rot on the ground as a mulch? No! Remove the falling fronds and burn them – this way you will remove the asparagus beetle.

In the second year of growth, take just a few spears as they appear like fat pencils. In the following year take 25%, and in the next year (and every year thereafter) take a third.

This is a long term crop – get it right and you will have super spears for years.

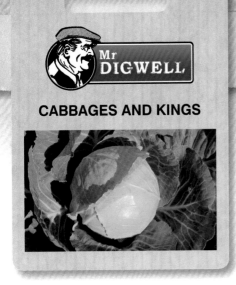

CABBAGES AND KINGS

Brilliant brassicas

We eat more brassicas than we think. They are not just sprouts and cabbages, cauliflowers and swedes, but include other plants such as watercress. Apart from grass, on which our animals feed, brassicas are our most important crop.

Clubroot

Way back, we didn't understand clubroot. We thought it happened because the soil was too acidic, but we were wrong. Affecting all the brassica family, clubroot is actually a fungal infection. It make the root swell terribly, causing the plant to get no nourishment and to become deformed.

The fungus is transferred on the bottom of your boots, so get into the habit of not walking on the soil – always use a plank. It helps to add lime to the soil – in quite large quantities and by using organic solutions.

If you grow all your brassicas in pots with a good trowel full of lime, and then put more lime into the soil when you transplant them, the fungus can't get to the roots until the plant is fairly mature.

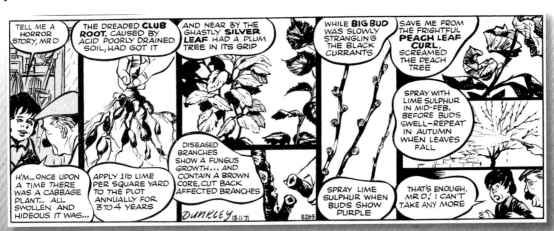

Pests

Brassicas suffer from many pests, most important of all – caterpillars. You can spray these insects, but I prefer to cover my crop with horticultural fleece. If you can, leave a sacrificial plant to encourage wildlife – we all need to be green!

Summer cauliflowers

I have sown cauliflowers in trays and transplanted them as you see in the cartoon. But the use of modules for all brassicas has transformed their growth. Sow a couple of seeds to each module and then discard all but the fastest growing plantlet.

In May or June put these plants into 15cm pots by pushing the plug out and transferring the plug (and the roots) to its final growing position. Many people complain to me they find cauliflowers difficult to grow, but with enough water and plenty of nutrients they will do well.

Swedes

Swedes take a long time to develop, but they take little work as they simply sit in the ground and grow. I grow them in small pots from seeds sown in modules and give them a little lime – though they are less prone to clubroot. They are completely frost hardy and can be left outside, but if they are continually frosted, they develop fibrous tissue and become less pleasant to eat.

QUICK TIP: *The old adage was, for every swede grow four turnips.*

Broccoli

Like all the brassicas, broccoli is one of the easiest plants to grow in the garden. Sow in modules in spring and discard all but the fastest growing per cell. Then transplant the

plants into their growing positions in the summer, using a lot of lime to combat clubroot, and harvest from late autumn to next spring.

Plant them out like cabbages and keep the plants mulched during the summer, and when the heads form take them just as they are tight, not all loose and blown. However, don't throw them away – they make brilliant soup.

Cabbages

Cabbages are one of the staples – you can have cabbages in the ground in every month of the year. Sowing in spring, summer and autumn, there isn't a month to be without them, but you actually don't need so many of them. Half a dozen sown for each season is fine. Start with summer cabbages now and then sow autumn cabbage in June, and spring cabbage in July/August.

In April you sow winter cabbage, and these will last you from November to spring – so when the bad weather comes, pop a cloche over them.

QUICK TIP: *The variety 'All Year Round' will give you cabbages at any time, which are not too large and have reasonably compact heads. If all you have is a small garden, these will grow in containers.*

Always remove the roots from the soil and burn them to stop the clubroot spores filling your compost.

Spring to Summer

As soon as we reach this time of the year the rush is on. Sometimes it seems like other gardens are further on with more developed plants, but keep an eye on the old gardeners, they know that the gardening year is not a sprint, it is a slow jog. Don't be tempted to get too much in the ground too soon – April and May can be very frosty at times.

Of course, there are plenty of things to be getting on with, and there are not enough hours in the day for seed sowing, pricking out, potting on, and finishing the last preparations of the beds and the lawn.

While a garden at this time of year has less to look at there are some joys to see – my favourite is the early clematis 'Montana', which always gladdens my heart and tells me there is hope of great things to come later in the year.

It's important to remember that while it may be shirt-sleeve weather in the garden, a few inches into the soil it can still be very cold. So if you are looking to harden off plants by taking them outside during the day and popping them back at night then help them along by warming the soil with a cloche or black plastic.

In this section

April

There is a lot of planting going on in the April garden. At last it feels like some progress is being made – dirty fingernails are the order of the day.

Planting bedding plants in borders is quite easy as they are planted very shallow. Indeed, you don't have to plant them at all, just cut round the module they came or grew in and plant so that nothing is peeping out of the soil.

Alpines are planted even shallower, often pushed between rocks or in indentations of pebbles. If you plant them in soil, they always look better with a covering of shingle.

Planting bulbs is easier with a bulb planter. Most of them like to be planted at just over a hand's length deep each – make this half as deep for smaller bulbs.

Shrubs and trees need a big hole, which has plenty of organic material for the plant to grow into. Notice that the roots spread out to the width of the plant, so try to imagine the plant in six months' time – that's how wide the hole needs to be.

Week by week

It is all too easy for the gardener to get carried away in April – remember the frosts can come and destroy all your hard work. If you sow, indoors or out, make sure the seedlings are protected. April is a month of preparation – have your compost, seed trays, pots and all plants ready and waiting.

Week 1

Continue to sow bedding plants, in particular marigolds, lobelia, nepetia, annual dahlias and salvia

Sow later tomatoes and capsicums

Plant potatoes

Sow cabbages, carrots, turnips, parsnips

Deadhead any remaining spent flowers

Week 2

Pricking out and potting on as necessary

First cut of the lawn

Start first peas

Prune shrubs that have flowered already

Give your carrot bed a good hoeing

Week 3

Sow broad beans in double rows

Sow salads in modules

Lift and divide spring bulbs

Prick out tomato seedlings

Week 4

Earth up any emerging potatoes

Give the hedges their first trim

Prune out and reseed herb beds as necessary

Cut back excessive growth on roses if the spring is warm

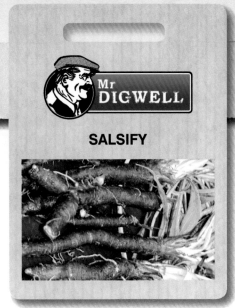

SALSIFY

In growing terms this plant is a combination of the carrot and runner bean. But in botanical terms it is more like a parsnip. Salsify has an unusual sweet oyster flavour, and is therefore good with fish, and sliced in stir-fries.

Dig a trench that is one spade wide and two spades deep. Mix half the soil you dig out with an equal amount of well rotted manure and fill the trench with it. Cover the trench with black plastic to warm the soil.

Give the soil/manure mixture a good hoeing and remove the stones – otherwise you will get a split root here and there.

In April, make a drill, which is a single scrape in the soil about 6cm deep, and sow thinly in this, one seed every few centimetres. The seeds should germinate within a week and you will need to continually thin until you have one plant every 20cm or so. The rows, if you need more than one, should be 30cm apart.

Lift in October – check you have decent-sized roots by scraping away at the soil. Salsify keeps quite well, but will deteriorate if left in the ground. Store on a shelf – I have found this to be much better than a pile or clamp.

GLOBE ARTICHOKES

Globe artichokes

This large thistle would be worth growing for its flowers alone. However, before the flower appears we can take the bracts that are closed and tight and they are delicious. Once the flower has opened it is too late!

I have long given up trying to grow these plants from seed. It takes too long and you have to keep them for a full year, and the following year take no flowers. It is much better, and easier, to buy ready rooted plants from the garden centre and plant them in April.

They need a lot of organic material and plenty of water. Plant them deep into well-dug soil and, if necessary, give them support with a cane.

In the first year let the plants grow, and remove the flowers before they can develop and compost them. But in the second year take them for the kitchen.

Pick the terminal bud first then the others as they appear. Remember, they need to be tight and full, but not open.

Globe artichokes are not related to Jerusalem artichokes in any way.

CELERY

Celery and celeriac

Some people think it's a lot of effort to create a vegetable that offers fewer calories when eaten than it takes to eat it. But to my mind that completely misses the point. Celery is not just a plant for slimmers to dig into their cottage cheese, it is a delicacy in its own right.

Where would a soup be without celery? For me this reason alone makes it worth going to all the trouble of growing it.

Celery is one of those plants that like a lot of nutrients. I have said it time and again, if a plant has to develop either a strong colour or a strong flavour it usually needs a lot of nutrients to do so. Celery is no exception.

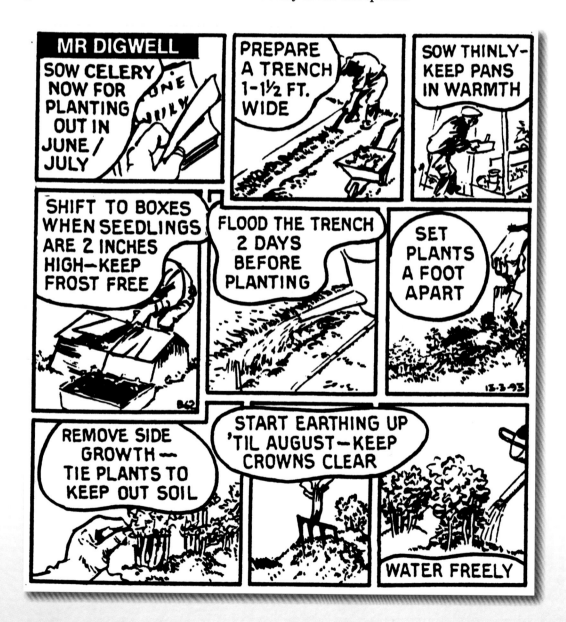

You start with a trench that is at least two spades deep and two spades wide. This will then be half filled with really good quality well rotted manure and topped up with soil and manure mixed.

Dig the trench in the winter, so long as the ground is amenable, and cover with plastic to keep the rain from leaching all those nutrients.

In April, sow seeds in a warm (about 15°C) greenhouse or windowsill. I now sow in large modules and let the plants grow to their planting-on stage, which is about a hand's length in size.

I do still very much believe in flooding the trench before planting: it helps young roots to get a head start – remember, when you transplant, you always kill some roots. It also takes time for the rest of them to recover, and if they look like they're drying out, give them plenty to drink.

Earthing up

This is the process of keeping light from the stems so they stay white. Tie the plants up to keep soil out from between the leaves and then draw soil around them with a draw hoe. Equally you could cut down a washing up bottle (the round ones – they were always round in my day) and slip a collar round the growing plant – it works just as well as soil.

There are some self-blanching varieties available, such as 'Golden Self Blanching'.

Celeriac

Celeriac used to be called celery root, and this is more or less what it is. It is a very swollen and ugly looking root, and is used in many ways in the kitchen: from sliced and boiled to mashed.

It is grown more or less in the same way as celery, but you don't have to bother with a trench as well-manured soil will do. Celeriac is less prone to drying out than celery, but as it grows the outer leaves can die off and get messy, so it is best to remove them.

Making a patio

The patio is increasingly an extension of the home, a kind of halfway house between the inside and the garden world. For some the patio is just about all the garden they have or at least it's a major part of it. For me, the patio is a place to grow more plants, by putting them in containers, as well as a place for a jolly good sit-down.

Creating a patio gives you plenty of topsoil for the rest of the garden. Whenever I have made one it has been a huge task to get rid of it all, so make sure you account for it in planning. Also siting your patio needs careful consideration. They do not have to be sited at the back door or French windows – think creatively!

Actually, a patio can be built anywhere in the garden as it is really just a very wide path, and it can be a great place to enjoy plants in shade or sunlight. Why not create a clematis-covered pagoda, or have a handkerchief tree hanging over a delicately shady seat?

Lay your patio on hardcore or broken bricks that are about 20cm deep, well bashed down to make a firm bed. You might want to use shuttering – a wooden frame to work to. This way it is easier to level your sand or concrete layer.

Use my way of making a path as a guide.

Planting in containers

There are plenty of plants you can grow in containers, which can make up the edges of your patio. You could easily build a low brick wall, two or three courses, coped but leaving a space for planting.

As well as flowers, why not plant some fragrant herbs: rosemary, lavender and sage. And don't forget night-scented stocks. I say this because I owe my great longevity to falling asleep to the multiple aromas of all these plants around me.

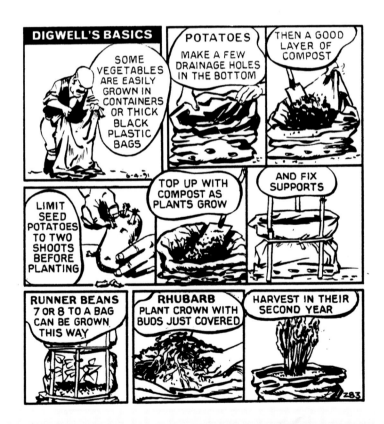

Growing vegetables on the patio

If it will grow in the ground, it will grow in a pot or container. All you need to remember is that the plants will need watering regularly to keep them from drying out.

There are good reasons for growing many plants in pots – you can move them around to follow the sun, you can put them near walls or shade, and you can change the look if you get fed up staring at the same ones. In many ways the patio is an ideal solution to the space-strapped garden.

PRIMULAS

You really cannot do without summer bedding – always plan to sow more than last year! You simply cannot get enough marigolds, for instance. I plant them all over the garden, between all kinds of vegetables and in the greenhouse and polytunnel too as they help combat certain plant pests and diseases.

Primulas

What a wonderful gardening world we live in. We no longer have to cover boxes of primulas with panes of glass! I used to have a stack of them, mostly broken cloche panes or greenhouse panes – they were all dangerous and I cut myself often. When the seeds go red, you know you have cut yourself!

I now sow primulas and most other bedding in a seed tray with a plastic propagator lid, and very recently under heat in a wonderful propagator.

I use an old coffee tin into which I put my seeds and a couple of handfuls of compost and pop the lid on. Then the whole thing is shaken up to mix the tiny seeds and spread them on top of the damp compost in the tray.

Then I prick them out into large modules when they are in full leaf. It takes a while, especially for the numbers I grow, but what else is April for?

Sweet peas

I don't suppose many people think of sweet peas as bedding plants, but they surely are, albeit they are a bit tall. They are basically used in beds, often at the back, and trained on a wall or trellis.

It's best to start them off in April, although you can overwinter them from an autumn sowing. The tip in the cartoon to cut out the growing tip allows for a bushier plant with more flowers.

Perhaps the best reason for growing sweet peas is the fragrance, which, like the colours, is best described as pastel.

QUICK TIP: *Soaking seeds is really important, you get better germination!*

Begonias

Begonias, especially the double varieties, have vibrant colours. Some call them gaudy, but I love 'em! They are a little temperamental when it comes to germination – keep the propagator lid on. I have a shelf system for seedlings, and the begonias go on the bottom in the shade – they come on better than if they are in the sunshine.

Phlox

Another plant not referred to as a bedding plant but which you can treat as such – dividing them up each spring for potting on and planting out – is phlox. It comes in all kinds of varieties and forms, some erect, others creeping. It is almost true to say you could populate the garden just with phlox and not get bored!

IRISES

The fantastic wet soil iris stands like a flag, which is its folk name. The 'Yellow Flag' is a wonderful wild plant, growing in clumps near rivers and ponds. I must say I adore the vivid yellow-marked deep-blue flowers of my Dutch varieties.

Irises propagate themselves naturally by sending out underground stems like rhubarb. An underground stem is called a rhizome, and has two functions. Firstly it stores a lot of food, mostly as starch. Secondly, at intervals along the rhizome a bud will grow into a new plant – just like a bud will make a new branch on a stem in the air.

So if you dig up your irises after they have flowered, you will find a thick rhizome at the end of it. You can cut pieces of rhizome, about 6cm long, and dip the cut surface into hormone rooting powder. This will not actually help with rooting, but it contains a fungicide that stops the pieces rotting. If you cannot get hormone rooting powder use sulphur powder.

Place the pieces into compost and they will soon root. You need to keep the compost a little damp – but water from below. Splashes can cause rot and the whole experiment will fail.

Once the plant has sent out a shoot, keep it in a cool, frost-free place until next May, when you can plant it out.

Try the same with other rhizomes; rhubarb, in particular, works well.

Making a lawn

My love affair with grass started when I was put in charge of a football pitch. Each spring I had to patch the whole pitch with new grass. My boss insisted I used a hand hoe to break up the soil. It took three months to complete the job, but boy we had good grass!

The problem with new gardens, those attached to new houses, is that the builders simply bulldoze the land flat, dump about four inches of topsoil on the rubble and then turf the lot. With a month of summer heat, the grass is dead.

Laying a lawn from grass seed is not as daunting as you might think – and certainly you get better results than with turf. On the whole, turf is cut from fields and contains all kinds of weeds. The higher quality turf is a lot more expensive than seed, and still you don't get the right finish.

Types of seed

Seed is not just one type of grass: the types are blended to create a lawn with specific qualities. You can get fine seed to make a fine lawn, which cuts very short and colours up beautifully. You can get a heavy duty seed mix for playing sports, or for children so they can run all day on it and not kick it up. You can even get shade lawn seed for gardens where the lawn is under a tree or by a wall.

You can also mix seeds to cope with your different circumstances. For example, the cricket wicket and the outfield, or the fairway and the green.

May

The May garden is becoming mature – well in as much as a teenager thinks it's mature. Plants are growing, flowers are opening and there is activity in the garden. However, I often think of May as a crocodile month. There are hidden dangers from late frosts, lurking insects and dozens of pests.

First of all May is the time for protecting what is already growing in the garden, the plants you have set into growth, the trees and fruit bushes. A feed of organic fertilizer now makes all the difference and brings on a spurt of growth.

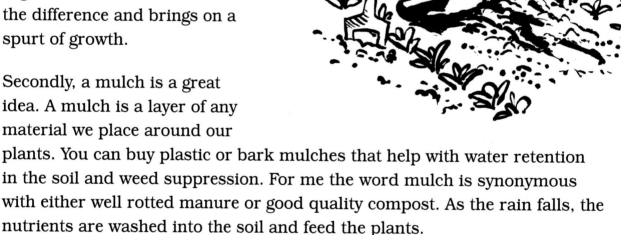

Secondly, a mulch is a great idea. A mulch is a layer of any material we place around our plants. You can buy plastic or bark mulches that help with water retention in the soil and weed suppression. For me the word mulch is synonymous with either well rotted manure or good quality compost. As the rain falls, the nutrients are washed into the soil and feed the plants.

As plants grow, so do the insects that feed on them. There are gentle ways of keeping our crops clean, ones that do not get into the food chain and accumulate in birds' eggs or human skeletons.

For my money a gardener will be wise if he spends some money on horticultural fleece, which causes no environmental problems, except, perhaps, in its manufacture.

Week by week

Perhaps the busiest month of the year, May sees the garden beginning to blossom. There is much to get on with – sowing out of doors, feeding perennials, and hoping the fruit has set in the spring. Seedlings grown indoors will need ventilating and watch out for the fungal infection "damping off".

Week 1

Sow vegetables outside – carrots, turnips, winter cabbage, French beans

Plant out bedding plants

Support tall plants like lupins and delphiniums

Mulch around plants in the herbaceous border with well rotted compost

Week 2

Softwood cuttings like fuchsia

Earth up potatoes

Sow salads outside

Feed spring bulbs – don't tie the leaves back

If you forgot – you can cut back shrubs like buddleia – to about five buds from the ground

Week 3

Cut the lawn lightly

Prune/trim the hedges

Hoe between onions and shallots

Thin out gooseberries

Plant mints in pots to keep them from taking over the garden

Week 4

Put straw under strawberries

Spray roses against black spot

Put your slug/snail controls in place

Plant out Brussels sprouts

Watch out – aphids appear this month

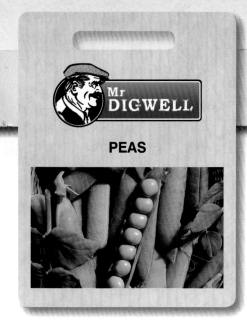

PEAS

Peas

When they first came to this country, some 250–300 years ago, peas were so popular that it's said they became "both a fashion and a madness". Reports exist of people eating so many peas straight from the pod they were ill, and guards were placed over fields. Today they are still one of our most popular vegetables.

Peas have come a long way in the garden and changed so much. The demands of combine harvesting huge fields of peas has meant the height of peas has reduced over the years, and now you will find it difficult to get the large vines of yesteryear.

Peas are easy-grow plants. Being legumes they are supposed to take nitrogen from the air and make nitrates, but they don't make that much and you certainly have to feed the soil before planting.

You can grow peas in all kinds of positions and places, from containers, pots and growbags to my favourite pea-growing trick – in a gutter. Fill the gutter with compost and allow a slow drip of water, which will feed them.

Apart from humans, there are lots of other animals fond of peas: pigeons are frequently the worst culprits but mice take quite a few too. I have found that netting them is the best answer, and I have stopped using mouse traps since, one day, I found a wriggling mouse in it. The poor animal must have been in agony for ages.

Sow them every three weeks from April to late August and you will have fresh peas in the pod from June to October.

PUMPKINS

Pumpkins

Around the country has sprung up the phenomenon of growing giant pumpkins for charity. There are weigh-off competitions, and people are sponsored for every pound or kilo the huge fruit weigh. You might think a pumpkin of 100 pounds was big, and it is, but monsters of over a thousand pounds are regularly grown and you wouldn't believe the lengths people go to hide them!

Actually, pumpkins are easy to grow. The keys to success are water, sunlight and feed. I don't often dig a hole and place manure in it to grow them these days. I just use a very rich mix of 50:50 soil and manure. I also start them off in pots indoors and transplant them.

Place the seeds in compost on their sides – this really is an important trick. You get much better germination that way.

How to grow a monster

Actually, genetics are important if you want to grow a huge one, but all pumpkins have the potential to weigh a few hundred pounds. All you have to do is feed them with a mixture of tomato feed and ordinary organic fertilizer, a cup in a litre of water, every couple of days.

Then water them every day. You might need to use a lot of water – from five to 20 litres a day depending on the weather.

You'll also need to keep the wind and rain off them – if you grow them in a polytunnel you are guaranteed to beat at least 100 pounds, if not more!

MARROWS

Outdoor marrows

What's the difference between marrows and courgettes? Not a lot really. Actually courgettes are slightly different and there is no truth in the idea that courgettes are young marrows. Well that's what the botanists say. Actually you wouldn't be able to tell the difference!

Marrows are best started off indoors and planted out at the end of May, in rich soil. But you can also sow them outside now. You can tell the difference between male and female flowers by the ovary at the back of the female one. You might get more males at first, but the female ones will soon catch up.

You can pollinate them yourself, and when the fruit starts to develop pull off the flower to avoid blossom end rot.

Like pumpkins, you will find success comes from water, feed and sunlight. Protect them from the rain and wind and you will soon be swamped with great green marrows.

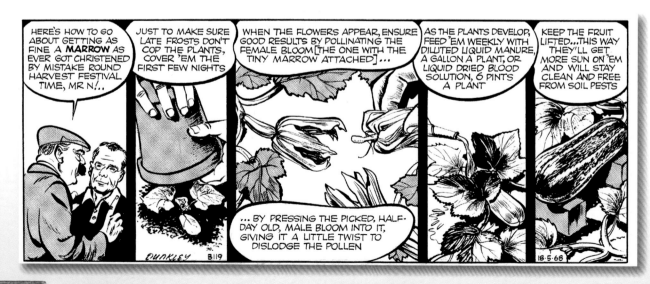

SWEETCORN

Sweetcorn

A journey along any motorway will be punctuated by fields of sweetcorn, even in the late autumn. However, although these plants do bear flowers, they will never fruit. They are destined to be harvested whole, chopped into little pieces and fed to milking cattle during the winter.

Sweetcorn is our largest cropping grass and it prefers a warm climate, and this is one of the problems growing it here in the UK. You will get the best growth in a polytunnel, but you need to keep both doors open to get a through draught in order to get proper pollination.

The reason for planting them in blocks is because sweetcorn are wind pollinated. If you planted them in a row, you might get no pollination at all, but in a block you should be fine.

Some varieties have multiple flowers and they should be restricted to about three per plant, otherwise the flavour will not be so good.

Harvesting them is a little more complex than just seeing the bracts go brown. Strip away the leaves and look for the corns. They should be milky yellow. Pierce a corn with the fingernail and they should be juicy and not hard. If not, leave them on the plant – they don't ripen off the plant so well.

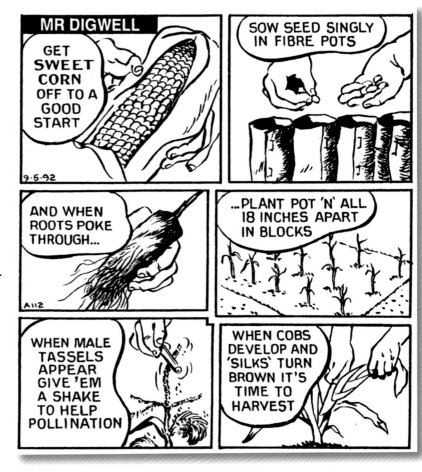

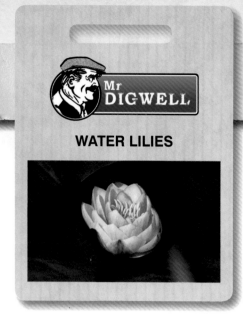

WATER LILIES

Water lilies

Apart from their absolute beauty, understanding water lilies allows us to gauge how deep water plants should be "planted". What is right for water lilies applies for many of the plants that are plunged into the water and appear at the surface.

Water lilies are "planted" in a special plastic container that looks a little like an old-fashioned shopping basket. This is lined and, surprisingly, filled with ordinary soil. This is then carefully plunged into the water to allow the plant to grow out. In the case of the lily, a long shoot reaches the surface, where the flower appears.

You can buy special fertilizer for those plants that need it – fertilizer that doesn't leach out into the water and cause a rapid increase in the algae population.

Different species prefer to be planted at their own specific depth, and this is achieved by carefully placing bricks or plinths in the water for them to stand on. However, you must be sure that whatever you use will not puncture the pond liner.

When it is time to divide the plants, you simply fish out the container and work on them, replacing the old soil with fresh before replacing the plant.

Be sure to leave any material you remove from the pond on the bank side so any organisms you have inadvertently taken out can get back!

MAY FLOWERS

May flowers

They follow April showers, do May flowers, and it is surprising how quickly May comes around and we are hardening off plants to cope with any last minute frosts. Believe me, over the years I have known it to snow in June!

Hardening off is the process of bringing plants out during the day to get them used to outdoor conditions. It is quite a shock, and they stop growing a little as a consequence. The outdoor temperature at noon is at least 5°C lower than indoors, but at night it is worse. So we bring them in for the night and take them out again for the following day. This continues for a week; at this time of year the days are more or less long enough so the night-time drop will not bother them too much.

Growing in modules makes it easier for the plants to be planted out. You simply push them from below and you have a perfect plug for growing.

CHICORY

Chicory

Chicory is a bitter leafy herb, much prized in France. So much that they used it as a herbal drink long before it was added to coffee. In Britain we have done much the same with dandelion, which is much better for you than either chicory or coffee. However, with good blanching chicory is very useful in the kitchen.

Sow in drills now and you will get good germination. Chicory plants need fairly fertile soil and will appreciate a foliar feed, that's one in which a liquid fertilizer is applied directly to the leaves, in July. Thin them out as they grow, to about one plant every 20cm or so. At the end of August, or early September, cover them with a pot, and be sure that the hole in the pot is covered so it is completely dark inside.

After about a month the leaves will be blanched. Leave one plant in the light as a comparison. Most of the bitterness will be gone and the roots can then be lifted.

Use the leaves in salads and the roots boiled. I knew a chap who used to dry both leaves and roots and smoke them in his pipe. Again, a French use that we copied with dandelions!

Mr DIGWELL

GLADIOLUS

Gladiolus

Glads were not invented in Australia, regardless of what Dame Edna might say. They are easy to grow, they have few predators, and are such a beautiful flower, so why they are not more widely grown I don't know.

I did say "glads" were easy to grow, but it wasn't until I used the sand trick that I had any great success. You see, most gardening books tell you to dig a hole and drop the corms in, and they do the rest. Not so!

Glads like a lot of water. Indeed, to grow prize specimens I dug a trench and half filled it with manure and spent compost to retain water. The results were poor, but putting a couple of inches of sand on the moisture-retaining material separated the corms and did the trick.

Some people plant glads with a bulb planter, which is fine, especially if you don't want them

in a line. I don't know what it is about glads that makes us plant them in regimented lines but try a trio of plants, a dahlia, a delphinium and a gladiolus, maybe in a planter. It truly is a wonderful effect.

Try to avoid lots of colours in one place. I prefer not to plant the variegated types.

The idea of the rose as England's national flower came about after the Wars of the Roses when the crown changed hands. It was a symbol that showed the union of the Houses of York and Lancaster. But something tells me that roses were loved long before the Middle Ages' propaganda machine got working.

The various types of rose each have their own requirements. First of all they all have a need of rich organic material, and consequently it is said they like to be mulched with well rotted horse manure. You would have thought that roses smell of horse manure in most growers' gardens, but of course roses are actually among the sweetest smelling flowers.

They prefer a mulch in the winter and this not only protects them – a warm blanket for the roots – it feeds them too. An extra summer top-up is welcome too.

Over the years the 'Hybrid Tea' has been the favourite type of rose, though modern versions of Old English roses are now giving them a run for their money.

How to buy roses

The golden rule in buying roses is to take your time. The photography in the catalogues is designed to show them in their best light. Go to specialist nurseries, during both summer and winter to see them actually growing, battling the elements and coping with the container. Note which ones have fungal infections and how they grow. You will then have a better idea about how they will cope in your situation.

Then order for a winter/early spring planting. Prepare the ground, adding a lot of manure to the soil a couple of months beforehand.

Deadheading

Use secateurs to remove flowers that are past their best. Doing this will change the hormone balance in the plant, which will then encourage more flower buds to develop.

How to prune a rose

Make cuts so that:

Branches are not touching

New branches grow outwards to create a dish shape

The cuts are just above a bud

Water does not fall on a bud

Try to remove buds that are subordinate to a three-bud tier. Where three flower buds form, the central one will usually be the best. Cut out the other two to encourage the central one to be even better.

Try not to let your roses wilt, it puts them under stress and they fall prey to other diseases. Black spot can be countered with copper-based fungicide. The other problem is aphid attack, which unfortunately can lead to all kinds of viral infections.

June

The garden in June has an air of business about it. For a start the insects have increased in number, and there are pollinators at every flower. The garden is alive with angry, protective black birds and fledgling tits seem to be arriving. In the sky the screams of martins make a warm day complete and a wet one all the more miserable.

June is a month of half-finished jobs in the garden. Many plants have started to grow and even flower but not all. Some, like aged daffodils and leaf-fallen clematis are past their best.

And there are more plantings to come. Yet more salads to replace those eaten by human and slug plus spring cabbages and spring bulbs!

Week by week

If there is one tool you use more than any other this month it is the hoe. Weeding becomes a part of life during the summer, closely followed by the secateurs and deadheading. Take away all the spent flowers and your prayers for replacements will likely be answered.

Week 1

Keep on weeding!

Trim back flowering shrubs and hedges

Trim laurel hedges, but not with clippers

Sow calendula in spare spots for late summer blooms

Week 2

Mow the lawn and give it a feed, repair patches

Harvest salads and Japanese onions

Tidy the plants in the pond area: warmth and water = plenty of growth

Build and fit hanging baskets

Week 3

Continue to plant summer bedding

Tie in canes of blackberries and remove raspberry suckers

Spray apples and other top fruit against fungal attack

Instigate aphid control

Week 4

Finally stop cutting asparagus

Continue to harvest strawberries

Feed fruit trees

Continue to earth up potatoes

TOMATOES

Tomato diseases

Tomatoes sown early in the year will now be producing fruit and this is where things start to go wrong. They can fall foul to all kinds of problems in the garden and greenhouse. The fresh air and slower growing outdoor tomatoes now start to catch up with the more disease-prone indoor ones.

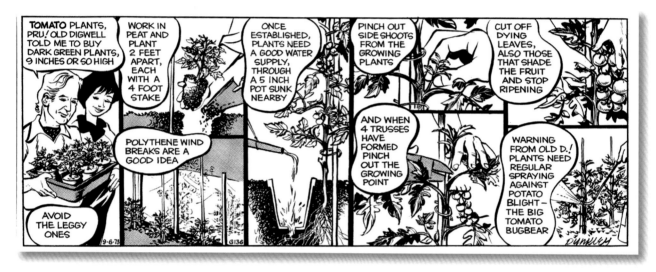

In the greenhouse, both warmth and humidity can lead to fungal infections. Therefore it's a good idea not to splash water about when watering tomatoes because it increases the humidity. Try watering in an empty pot next to the plant to avoid unwelcome splashes.

QUICK TIP: *While we're talking about watering, if you make your own fertilizer tea, try not to use it in the greenhouse on tomatoes – it is the biggest source of infection. Use bought tomato feed, which is just as good.*

Blight

Tomatoes and potatoes are members of the nightshade family and as such they both get blight. Try not to go from the potatoes to the tomatoes, especially if it is raining after a hot spell, and if you do wash your hands on the way. You can easily transfer blight from one to another.

Although you can spray against blight, personally I don't like to. Instead grow blight-resistant varieties like 'Cara'.

Although the cartoon says it, I have had next to no success using Bordeaux Mixture – a copper-based fungicide used for hundreds of years on grapevines. It does work well on other fungal infections, and I use it half strength once a week.

Flower dropping

This usually happens when the plant is too dry, but can happen when it is too wet too. If you are growing in a growbag, remember to pierce all around to give the bag good drainage. If you have neglected your toms so they drop their flowers, it will be pretty hard to get them going again.

Dry set

This is when not enough pollen has fallen on the flower. Each of the seeds in the tomato needs a pollen grain to make the journey from the flower to the seed. Otherwise the fruit will not develop properly.

Blossom end rot

This is where the flower rots on the fruit, causing the bottom of the fruit to blacken. The fruit is inedible and wasted. It is caused by neglect – such as a lack of water for a time, then a gush of it to make up for the mistake. Always keep the water regular.

Splitting

Again, lack of water, then a gush causes the fruit to swell and then split. It is also, though more rarely, caused by excessive heat.

How to take cuttings

Imagine being able to cut your thumb off and then stick it somewhere else to grow another version of yourself. Well this is exactly what is happening in the plant world all the time. Taking cuttings is an excellent way to increase our stock.

There are many reasons why cuttings work. First of all there are so few plant hormones that the removal of a bud is, chemically, an important event. Secondly, in the wood there is a layer of cells called cambium, which are able to respond to the situation and grow new parts – for example a root.

The key to the situation is not letting the plant dry out and at the same time keeping it free from fungal infection. For this reason we remove many leaves, but not all, to cut down transpiration. Sometimes we also cover the plant with a plastic bag for the same reason.

We also use hormone rooting powder, mostly because it has a fungicide in it. The plant produces its own rooting hormones freely enough.

QUICK TIP: *The best part of the plant from which to take cuttings is where there's new growth.*

Taking cuttings is taking advantage of a plant's ability to rejuvenate after being partly eaten by a herbivore. Roots left in the ground simply grow new shoots. Perennial weeds can grow again from a centimetre piece of root or stem!

Nearly all shrubs and perennial herbaceous plants can be generated in this way – but sometimes you need to play the statistics game. From 10 cuttings you might find eight that you can take and grow into new plants. The older the wood the worse chance of success you have.

Perhaps the most readily propagated plants by this method are fuchsias. Using cuttings from this year's growth, they take very easily. Busy Lizzies and geraniums are excellent cutting plants too. You can try your hand and gain in confidence.

Lawn care

A lawn with weeds will eventually break down, leaving room for moss to grow that will dry out in the summer giving your lawn a patchy look to it. Regular mowing deals with most weeds, but the larger ones will need digging out, and the bare patch reseeding.

Another "weed" – moss

Grass is a remarkable plant. You can cut it to within a few millimetres of the ground and it will live quite happily, sending out rhizomes and filling the space available to it. But the problem is that grass dies and rots in situ, making a home for moss. When you get moss in the lawn, it is less rugged and people walking on it can damage it.

Also, in the summer, the moss dries out, again leaving a patch. So these patches have to be filled in with

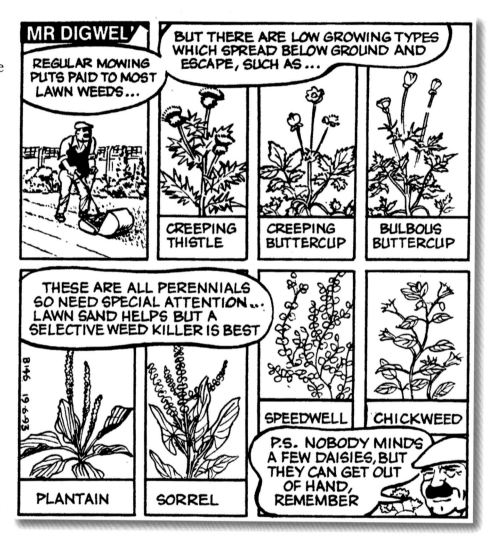

new seed. Hoe out the patch until it is fine and crumbly. If you know the type of grass you used all the better, because you can match the colour. It may come as a surprise to know that grasses come in different colours.

If you don't know the grass, then you need to over sow. That is, to sprinkle grass on the chopped up patch, and over a wider area to blend your new patch into the surrounding grass.

The way to avoid moss is to scrape out the dead grass twice a year – a process called scarifying. This is the main function of a tined grass rake.

Beetroot

BEETROOT

Beetroot is a wonderful plant, but just making all that colour takes quite a lot of work, added to which its strong flavour means it needs a lot of nutrients. If you get the basics right, you will never have any trouble with beetroot.

Despite what I used to say, I now sow beetroot right into July and cloche them in September. I also make use of the leaves – especially when young – and I have sown beet as late as September just for the salad bowl.

The reason for growing beetroot in rows is to make it easy to thin them out. They grow as much as they can until they touch each other, then they stop. So, regardless of how they are thinned, you always get the same weight of beetroot overall. You might have 20 small ones or 10 large ones.

These days people do not just grow beets for the swollen roots. They are used young as stir-fry ingredients, and in salads as already mentioned.

Beetroot is probably one of the most versatile plants we have!

Winter salads

You can have salads at almost any time of the year, so long as you make it warm enough for the plants to germinate. Most salad vegetables, apart from tomatoes, cucumbers and capsicums, are not particularly affected by the length of the day, so once you have got them growing they will give you a crop.

Swiss chard

You can get a lot of chards these days and they make great additional leaves in salads, chopped up. You can even slice the central stalk for a bit of a crunch.

To stop chards being bashed about by the wind, cover them with cloches and take one leaf from each at a time. This way, a row of them will last you right into the winter.

Endive

In the same vein, endive is another crispy and bitter salad vegetable that lasts into the winter. This one, like chicory mentioned earlier, is bitter and needs to be blanched. If you put it into darkness in September, it will be ready to eat a couple of weeks later. You can sow this plant right through to September too, and have a Christmas crop.

Lettuce

You can sow lettuce in every month of the year, as long as you keep it inside from November to March. It doesn't like being transplanted, though, and needs to be handled carefully. For this reason I invented what I call the "ring culture module". Take an ordinary module tray and sow lettuce seeds in compost. When they are about a hand's breadth high, carefully cut around each module with scissors and also cut out the bottom – being careful not to spill any compost. Then simply push them into an appropriate hole in the soil.

Carrots

Other winter favourites for salads must include carrots. I set them off in boxes in November in a warm greenhouse. They then provide a few dozen baby carrots at any time – perfect in salads!

Late summer sown carrots will provide maincrop-sized roots in September and October, quite easily.

Use any of the 'Early' varieties, like 'Early Nantes', because they need a shorter period to come to maturity and they are not so bothered by cold weather. You can sow every couple of weeks between July and the end of August, but don't thin the later sowings too hard.

Winter parsley

I love a few parsley leaves in a leafy salad and you can enjoy this all the year round. Actually, it was used by the Romans as a breath freshener – but then they also used garlic for the same job, so goodness knows how bad their breath was!

Parsley doesn't like having wet feet, and

since it is always wetter in the winter they need really well-draining soil – so provide some extra drainage by adding sand.

KNIPHOFIA

This page is a plea, one which I hope you'll forgive me for making. When I was young I was given a very old book on plants that was almost completely useless except that it contained a single photograph that somehow captured my imagination. It was a photograph of Mr Charles Darwin, with his long beard, examining a kniphofia in the herbaceous border of his garden.

The plea is to grow kniphofias!

This tremendous plant looks like a red hot poker – although in these days of central heating, people won't see the comparison so easily. It was actually named after Johann Hieronymus Kniphof, a German botanist.

Natives of South Africa, kniphofias like plenty of warmth and free-draining soil that can be moist in the summer, but must be drier in the winter. They actually grow high in mountains in the wild, so generally they do quite well in our climate.

You can get yellow ones, but these unusual lilies are mostly apricot/red, tipped with yellow. They are easily grown from seed and will clump up, so you can simply dig up a clump and divide them.

Shrubs to prune

You have frequently heard, no doubt, the phrase "Nature needs taming" in relation to pruning shrubs. Well, I understand what they mean, but it isn't really how it works. Many shrubs become long, leggy, woody and progressively lose their flowers if just left to their own devices.

The point is that in the wild these plants are subject to grazing animals, and pruning mimics this to a great extent.

Mock orange

This beautiful shrub needs cutting back after flowering, reducing the branches by a third. Without this treatment, the branches will become very woody and the flower buds will find it increasingly difficult to break through.

Do the same for lilac, which if left alone will have long poles of branches and not much else, so be cruel to be kind. Cut away at the flowered branches, and to achieve a good open shape. Typically, people are afraid of cutting back hard. If you don't, what happens is you end up with nothing more than a dead stick. Be bold and reduce the wood.

Summer to Autumn

The summer marks the height of the gardener's year; when our gardens reach maturity and are at their best. It's a time when the first job of every day is to enjoy what you and nature together have created. If gardening is only about doing things, the tasks and the processes of producing a garden, then it wouldn't be worth the job. To actually sit back and enjoy the aromas, the colours and the food has to be, for me at least, one of the main reasons to garden. So don't forget the value of a well-earned rest.

But the jobs still do catch up with us in the end. They fall into a number of categories – weeding, deadheading, watering and irrigation, pest watching and harvesting. Add to that the need to sow and plant winter vegetables, keep the greenhouse and polytunnel cool and you have quite a lot to do by any standards. Perhaps it's a good idea the days are longer in the summer because there is more to do.

It is at this time of the year that gardeners reflect on the past year. Some years apples ripen early, usually because of a mild spring and a warm but moist summer. Other years there seem to be lots of diseases – particularly when blight is prevalent when lots of rain follows a long, hot, dry spell.

Many horticultural societies have their annual show from September onwards – so there is plenty to do if you are to stand a chance of any prizes!

In this section

July

Some time in July the garden will be at its peak. Predicting when this will happen is almost impossible, but when it happens it will be stunning. You are looking to keep the garden in full colour, as well as being as productive as possible, but in the later part of the month you will have to work extra hard. Deadheading helps, as does summer feeding and maintaining the right water balance. Neither too much (which is wasteful) nor too little (which is equally wasteful) is a fine balance to achieve.

The most important thing about the July garden is you learn a lot about how your garden, and the plants in it, react to the height of the summer. Let's hope it's a positive reaction!

QUICK TIP: *In periods of drought, and probably therefore a hosepipe ban, use the hoe around plants to increase the evaporation of topsoil water. It sounds crazy, but Victorian gardeners used this trick to draw replacement water from below. It only works for so long though!*

Week by week

During July there are many conditions that cause it to start that slow decay towards autumn. Much of the time can be profitably spent deadheading. When you take a spent flower away from a plant the hormone balance is changed and the result is more flowers! You can keep some plants going right into October by deadheading.

Week 1

Plant out young plants into final bed/pot position

Remove spring bulbs from the soil and leave to dry out after foliage has died back

Cut back early flowering plants and water well

Hoe borders to keep weeds back

Week 2

Sow courgettes, marrows and sweetcorn

Check potatoes for blight if wet, water well if dry

Uncover and bed down strawberries using fleece and straw

Sow runner beans

Week 3

Harvest early potatoes once first flowers are out

Sow climbing French beans

Check beds for weeds, removing as much as you can

Encourage sweet peas to climb by tying to canes

Week 4

Plant out tomatoes and tie to canes

Check if early peas are ready for harvest

Check roses for black spot and aphids

Sow salad crops

JAPANESE ONIONS

Japanese onions and winter sowings

There are two onion crops in the year, one from seeds sown in late December (or sets in April) and one from sets planted more or less in July and August. These latter onions are from Japanese stock, and they take advantage of late summer sunshine to get themselves into a position to overwinter.

Onion sets that are pushed into the ground by using the onion itself as a dibber come out of the ground more readily as the roots grow. It is much better to make a hole with a dibber – a finger will do – and firmly set the onion in place, then firm it in too. This way you won't get many escapees, and the birds are less likely to pull them up.

Sowing spinach, and any other greens like spring cabbage, is easy in July because the soil is warm and they get off to a flying start. Don't bother to sow in pots now, but remember that they do prefer lime, so give 'em lots.

MR DIGWELL

'JAPANESE' ONIONS CAN BE SOWN IN AUGUST FOR AN EARLY HARVEST

TRY 'ISHIKURO'—IT WON'T FORM BULBS

THE COLOUR OF 'SANTA CLAUSE' MAKES FOR AN EYE-CATCHING SALAD

THEY CAN BE PULLED AT ANY SIZE FROM PENCIL THIN TO LEEK SIZE

MAKE A SOWING OF WINTER SPINACH TOO THIS MONTH! SPACE SEED 1 IN. APART

THIN SEEDLINGS TO 2 IN. APART —THEN IN EARLY SPRING TO 6 IN.

LET PLANTS GET FAIR-SIZED BEFORE YOU START PICKING

HARVEST OUTER LEAVES WHILE THEY'RE STILL YOUNG AND TENDER

Japanese onions are harvested at any time, but cloche them in December and if you can wait till May you'll have a bumper crop.

SPRING BULBS

Spring bulbs

How magnificent is gardening! In mid summer you are surrounded with perfection, colour, form and texture, and yet you are thinking of brightening up an otherwise drab garden covered in frost, or worse, shrouded in rain and darkness. It's time to get planting those spring bulbs.

Another way of planting bulbs is to use a bulb planter. This pulls a plug of earth and grass out of the lawn and you can place the bulb at the appropriate height in a soil and compost mixture. The plant will push through the hole. If you really want to you can put a sprinkling of grass seed on the top of the compost and water it in. I have found the grass actually fills the space anyway.

One problem with this approach is the walls of the hole – they are a bit stiff and solid, and the bulb finds it a little more difficult to reproduce itself, so chop at the sides of the hole a little when planting.

If you are going to plant snowdrops and bluebells, be sure to buy local, British plants. Interbreeding between garden and wild specimens is changing the natural wild plants.

MR DIGWELL — WHEN CROCUSES APPEARED ON THE LAWN SPRING WAS ON THE WAY! SO PLANT SOME NOW — LIFT AND FOLD BACK A SQUARE OF TURF — SET BULBS 2 INS. APART, 3-4 INS. DEEP — THEY LOOK GOOD AROUND TREES, SHRUBS — COLOURS AVAILABLE ARE FANTASTIC — SAME TREATMENT APPLIES TO DAFFODILS — SNOWDROPS — SCILLAS — GRAPE HYACINTHS — LEFT UNDISTURBED THEY SPREAD THEMSELVES!

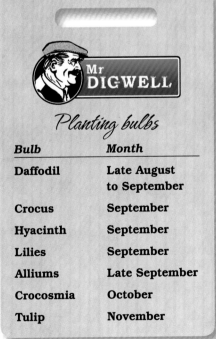

Planting bulbs

Bulb	Month
Daffodil	Late August to September
Crocus	September
Hyacinth	September
Lilies	September
Alliums	Late September
Crocosmia	October
Tulip	November

WISTERIA

Wisteria

Wonderful wisteria! There is nothing else to describe it, the huge flower stalks falling from the side of a cottage is usually the way people are first introduced to this plant. There are a few things to remember about this plant, including the fact it is a greedy grower. One last thing, if a plant name ends in "ia" it usually means it is named after someone, and in this case it is Charles Wister, an American merchant.

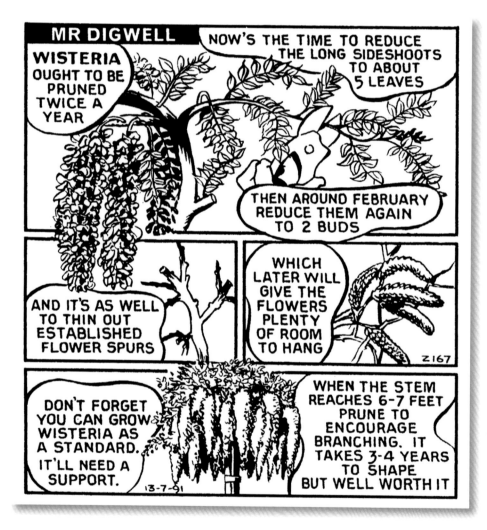

Wisteria is a forest plant that roots itself in the forest floor but climbs over trees. As the wisteria grows it finds a tree branch to climb on, as it grows it turns clockwise until it has a good grip. It likes a lot of nutrients and needs regular feeding: at least a good mulch in the spring and perhaps an organic feed in water in the summer.

Training a wisteria

You are looking to train the side branches more or less horizontally, so that they are not drooping or vertical. This way you get more flowers. Cut back the leaf-bearing branches, leaving only three to five leaves on each, and in the winter cut them back again to a couple of buds.

Any branches that do not look as though they are going to produce good horizontal growth should be cut out completely.

Support

Don't underestimate the weight a wisteria puts on your building. The largest one in the world weighs over 250 tonnes, and even a small one can be quite a burden. I have a friend who says the only thing holding his cottage up is his wisteria. Be sure you can take the weight, and consider an extra wooden support. They get so big and strong that they will easily crush a tree – so it is preferable they are not allowed to climb over your garden trees, and they are kept away from telegraph poles and television aerials.

The flowering spurs emerge along the branches and are frequently impeded by old flowers, so after they have flowered and are looking a little ragged, cut them off.

Always buy container-grown plants with a good graft, and watch out for the new wisteria beetle, moving up from the south!

CLEMATIS

Clematis

Some of our most beautiful flowers are borne by climbers and clematis is no exception. They come in three forms, early flowering, mid flowering and late flowering, and each one has to be treated differently. They will grow in almost any soil, but one common factor is they like to have cold feet. That is to say, place some pebbles around the base of the plant and they will grow much more happily.

No pruning clematis

This applies to the following plants:

C. alpina,

C. chrysocoma,

C. macropetala,

C. montana,

C. cirrhosa and

C. armandii.

If you prune them they are likely to die. Only give them the lightest of trims to keep them in order.

Light pruning clematis

If your plant flowers in May and June, it is best only to prune it lightly. Find the end of a branch and take it back to the next but one branch.

Hard pruning clematis

These plants flower later in the year on new growth. Prune in February and start at the base of the plant. Go up the branch to a couple of buds and prune just above that – the plant will produce lots of new growth and thence lots of flowers.

CAMELLIAS

Camellias

Camellias can be the most frustrating plant in the world. The promise of wonderful blooms is witnessed by everyone as the fat flower buds form in September but the frost kills them so frequently. When your flowers open in the spring and they are stained brown, that is frost damage. The plant itself is quite hardy, but the flowers certainly are not.

For this reason I have started to keep my camellias in pots and large tubs so I can drag them into a cool but frost-free greenhouse for the worst of the weather, and take them outside again in April.

Grow them in ericaceous compost as they like an acidic soil and not too many nutrients. Give them a late winter feed of well rotted compost and perhaps a liquid feed in the summer. You can buy special acidic fertilizers for ericaceous plants. This is especially needed if you are growing in containers. Camellias respond well to pruning, and you can cut them back hard to rejuvenate a plant that has seen better days.

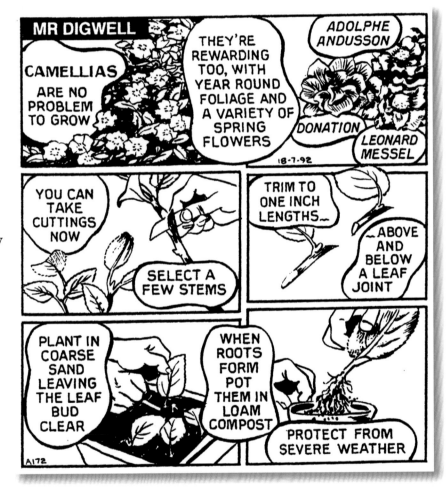

Don't forget to trim the roots if you are cutting your camellia right back and repotting it.

CARNATIONS

Layering carnations

Carnations and pinks don't send out runners like strawberries, but they do respond to a similar treatment when it comes to propagating new stock. I do love these delicate plants, they are called pinks, and I believe there is a bit of misunderstanding about the name.

The word Dianthus (carnations and pinks) is translated as "pale rose colour" and, for unknown reasons as small – consequently our little finger is known as a "pinkie". So, contrary to popular belief, the pinking shears that cut a serrated edge were named after "pinks" or Dianthus, and not the other way round.

Layering is an ancient technique, and it is surprising how

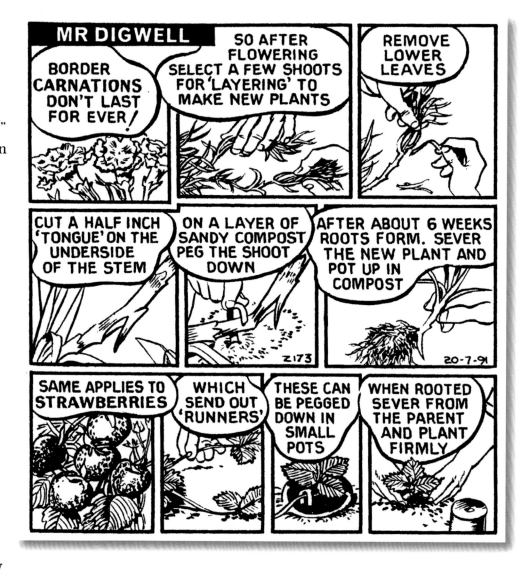

many plants take to it. Most of our hedgerows are treated in the same way, cutting halfway into the stem and bending it over. It is best if you can use hoops to hold the plant in contact with the ground rather than a pebble – which is what I use with strawberries.

HEATHERS

Heathers

I was once passing a row of terraced houses, each with a small garden, and was amazed to see the finest display of heather I ever witnessed. Packed into an area of about 10 square metres there were so many different colours and plants; when I asked permission to photograph them the lady said there were 32 varieties that had been planted by her husband some years earlier.

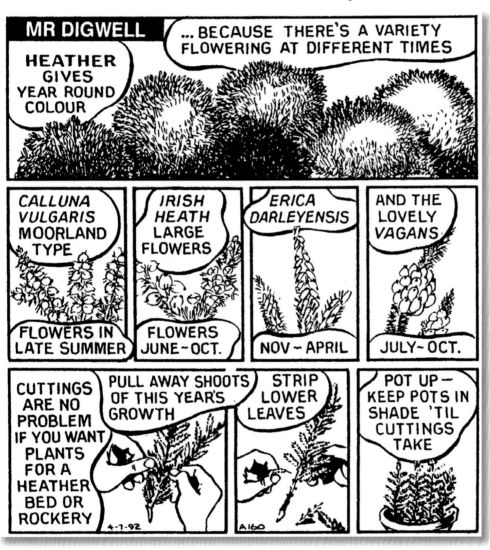

Ericas

Heathers belong to the genus Erica, and are acid-loving plants of bog and moorland. They are the original ericaceous plants after which we named the acid-loving group.

Tremendously easy to grow, they can withstand cold and wet, some measure of drying out, lack of nutrients and complete neglect. However, they do have a tendency to be woody, and need trimming regularly to encourage new growth as opposed to beefing up the twigs that are already there.

The only real proviso for heathers is they get full sun and face south. This seems to be a little counterintuitive when you consider where they come from, but they certainly don't do well in the shade.

Dealing with pests

I might be banging the drum a bit, but it is important to point out how much things have changed for gardeners. These days we should stick to a single, golden rule. If it ain't natural, don't do it!

Hindsight

The advice in the above cartoon would get me arrested now, but way back it was fine to use DDT and Aldrin. They have been banned because they are responsible for all kinds of genetic mutations, particularly soft shells in birds eggs.

But, looking back on it we didn't have to use the stuff. Gardeners for centuries never used such harsh chemicals on the land. It became a way of thinking that swept away all the good stuff we had learned about how to garden. Just because we are told it was OK – did we have to believe it?

So what are the options for gardening with compassion these days?

Making a start

I am not expecting you to completely stop spraying or using chemicals, just be a little more savvy when you do. Take slugs as an example. Everyone has their own system for dealing with slugs. We have gone from the blue pellets to using all kind of different treatments – beer traps, eggshells, nematodes that blow them up from the inside, and even rolled up sheep's wool.

The point is that, for slugs, no matter how many you took out with pellets there was a considerable army to replace them. So what's the point? The name of the game is now protecting your plant, and living with slugs rather than fighting against them.

Being responsible

There are times we have to spray, otherwise there would be no crops at all. This applies particularly to fruit but even then we can spray responsibly. Not spraying plants in flower, for example, means the bee population is saved from a dramatic poisoning. And remember, a bee will take that poison back to the colony!

Working with nature to encourage a good balance of fauna is the best way to garden. If, for example, you wipe out all the pests in the garden, something else will come and replace them. Living with them is much easier and with practise you get great results.

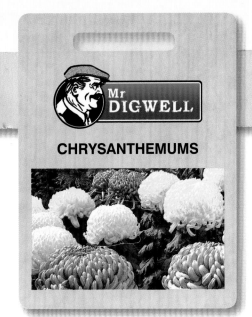

CHRYSANTHEMUMS

Chrysanthemums

These popular and beautiful flowers get their name from the Greek words for 'gold flower' yet today they come in all kinds of colours. In Britain they are at their best just as the weather is at its worst, so make sure you take extra care to have them looking their best as they help add colour to the garden when it most needs it.

As a rule, chrysanthemums are fairly hardy plants, but they do need a bit of care in the bad weather. They should be sown in early spring under cover, and should be potted on in a good quality compost and kept in a cold frame or in a nice, sheltered spot.

Plant them out into their final growing positions with a cane for support as high winds can damage the stems very easily. When they are approximately nine inches tall take off the tips of the plant to encourage side shoots and maximum blooms. Make sure the weeds are kept at bay and keep them well watered in dry spells.

Chrysanthemums will grow in parts of the garden that other plants don't work in as they are not too fussy about soil type or light levels. If you keep them fed and regularly deadheaded, they will flower from the end of summer right through to the early winter months, providing you with a show as everything else dies back.

When they have finished flowering, cut them back so they will flower again in the spring.

Crocuses

CROCUSES

I don't know if you have noticed it but a crocus peeping through the snow always has a melted ring around it. It is almost as though it has some warmth inside, and that's how it makes me feel! Actually, crocuses do have some antifreeze in their outer cells, and this melts the snow.

Crocuses grow best in sandy soil and bright sunny conditions. Plant them in August and they will be strong enough to thrive when the colder conditions return in late autumn. On the whole they are easy plants to grow, and they thrive in the cold. They stand up better than their larger cousins, colchicums – you hardly ever see them flopped over on the ground.

Crocuses do equally well in pots, but to my mind there is nothing more thrilling to see a snow-whitened lawn with lots of blue or yellow crocuses peeping through.

In September, give them a liquid feed, that's all they need really.

They propagate themselves by reseeding, and you can dig the first season plants and move them about – repotting them to give more room.

Apart from falling asleep in the deckchair on the patio and sipping cooled mint tea from the herb garden, August can be a difficult month. You often get requests to water other people's gardens while they are away, or asked "... will you just look after my tomatoes?" and so on. Well that might be well and good, but there are lots of things to be getting on with in my own garden thank you very much.

One of the great joys of the August garden is preparing for the spring, and this month I will be starting off a whole new batch of freesias, which will bring complete delight when they flower and disperse their aroma in the winter.

For gardeners it is always important to plan ahead, yet as you pass through the seasons your garden passes with you. Another way of looking at it is that we have a number of different gardens that are constantly changing, and "getting close to nature" is best achieved in a garden than anywhere else. After all, so we are told, our first home was a garden.

Week by week

August is the best month in the year for discovering which areas of our gardens are the wettest. Having done so we can plan to put our most delicate plants in the area so that they will flourish even when it's dry and there's no water to be had.

Week 1

Keep all plants watered through dry weather, especially pots

Feed pot plants using tomato food

Deadhead flowers for prolonged shows

Continue to sow and plant out salad crops

Week 2

Trim bushes back to just behind the first leaves

Lift shallots and onions after leaves have wilted, and then dry and store

Earth up maincrop potatoes

Sow winter spinach

Week 3

Feed pot plants using tomato food

Use garden waste to make compost

Plant out daffodils and crocuses for next spring

Trim hedges

Week 4

Remove crops that have been harvested and enrich soil with manure or compost

Transplant cabbage and broccoli, watering well

Water plants, especially in dry spells

Harvest peas and beans

GERANIUMS

Geraniums

I fill borders, hanging baskets and containers with all kinds of geraniums. They are easy to grow, cheap to propagate and very colourful. To be honest, I find them somewhat intrusive, there is a pink one I don't know the name of that runs wild in the garden and is very difficult to get rid of. For this reason, I grow them in 8cm pots and bury the plant and pot together wherever possible.

Geraniums will grow almost in fresh air such is their grasp on life. Certainly cuttings take very quickly. You can dip them in rooting powder and plonk them into a bottle of water and you will see how rapidly the roots start to form.

I walk around the garden with a tray and whip off a cutting – at least one from every plant, and pot them on for next year's borders. But I always wear rubber gloves because the oils from the plant irritate my skin.

Keep them in a cool greenhouse over the winter and use them as you see fit next year.

Unusual containers

Planting in unusual containers is not only fun, it's frugal too. There are so many novel ways to brighten up a garden – you see a lot of this sort of thing on allotments rather than home gardens – we are a little too formal, usually, for that sort of thing at home.

I have grown carrots for showing in drainpipes. You have to cut the pipe in half lengthways and then tape it back together again. The pipe can be about two metres long. Then sow a couple of carrots in the top and while they are germinating, balance the pipe at a 45-degree angle. Remove all but the best growing carrot and store the pipe horizontally. Every day, turn the pipe by about an eighth. Over the months the carrot will grow to the bottom of the drainpipe, and when you cut the drainpipe open you will have a huge carrot.

Turnips in toilets, beetroots in boots, garlic in teapots, chives in coconuts – there are so many innovative ways to make a statement or have a laugh. Perhaps the best I ever saw were parsnips in a baby's pram.

MR DIGWELL

NEXT TIME YOU BUY FRUIT PACKED LIKE THIS

DON'T THROW THE NET CONTAINER AWAY LINE IT WITH SPHAGNUM MOSS AND FILL IT WITH COMPOST

SET IN CROCUS BULBS

SECURE AND FIX WITH A LOOP

GIVE IT A GOOD SOAK, BEFORE HANGING IT UP

AND IN DUE COURSE BULBS WILL SHOOT

AND GIVE YOU A SPLENDID SHOW AT CHRISTMAS

29-8-92

Don't throw anything away – grow a plant in it – but remember, be sure to have plenty of drainage holes.

CYCLAMEN

Cyclamen

As a child I saw a cyclamen and thought it was plastic. I tried to melt it. You can imagine my surprise as these are the most perfect flowers you can find. I once compared them to a "Punk Rocker's" hairdo – standing upright and purple/pink. Those found outdoors are not as delicate as they look, but are quite tough.

There are essentially three types of cyclamen, hardy ones, non-hardy ones and those in-between. Plants sold as house plant cyclamen will not survive the winter outside. Actually, the hardy ones really only tolerate the cold – they usually suffer ill effects from it, but recover reasonably quickly.

QUICK TIP: *Cyclamen come from beech woods and prefer partial shade. In the winter they appreciate any cover you can give them – a cloche is ideal.*

An essential is good drainage because cyclamen can rot when forced to live in wet. A handful of grit, mixed into the growing position, usually helps.

In order to grow perfect specimens, grow cyclamen in pots. A 15cm pot with two-thirds compost and one-third grit is super. They can be taken outside, even buried, pot and all, and then brought back indoors at the coldest times.

MR DIGWELL

IF YOU SOW CYCLAMEN SEED NOW...

...IN POTTING COMPOST – AND COVER...

...YOU'LL FIND SEEDLINGS WILL BE READY TO POT ON, SINGLY, IN ABOUT 6 WEEKS

MAKE SURE THE CORM SITS CLEAR OF THE COMPOST

REPLANT IN LARGER POTS AT THIS STAGE

BY DECEMBER YOU'LL BE ALL SET FOR A COLOURFUL CHRISTMAS

B 188   7-8-93

Sowing from seed

Cyclamen seeds can be difficult germinators. Firstly they need to be soaked in tepid water for 24 hours. Secondly they need to be in the dark – complete dark – until they actually start growing. They are then fairly easy to grow so long as you don't let the seedlings dry out. They don't need to be too wet, but they must never be dry.

Always start with fresh seed as they die very easily, or can germinate and then fall prey to damping off.

From the potting-on stage they are easy to handle and as long as you keep them within the parameters for that particular variety, you'll have great flowers around Christmas.

Old school shrubs

I just love my hebe, my hyperacid and fuchsia, but there are times when you just want a bit of scent as well as a lovely plant, and the following handful of shrubs are the best o' the bunch in my view.

Cistus is the gum cistus, which seems to hybridize with everything going. Its other name is rock rose, and it is as pretty as any wild rose. The five petals are dotted in the centre and the aroma is unforgettable.

Cytisus is another plant that hybridizes a lot. Otherwise known as brooms, they hybridize with laburnums and gorse.

Lonicera or honeysuckle is a wonderful climbing shrub, once smelt, never forgotten. Try putting a full flower in a glass of Pimms – marvellous!

Osmarea is a member of the oleander family, so you would imagine the aroma to be heady and wonderful, and so it is, heavy and jasmine, just the trick on a hot summer night.

Ulex is the gorse. It is said that kissing season extends to when the gorse is in flower – how fortunate that it is always in flower! The whole of Anglesey smells of gorse, a scent somewhere between bacon and eggs and vanilla.

HYPERICUM

Hypericum

This plant is known as the Rose of Sharon and, more commonly, as St John's wort. It forms close shrubs with yellow flowers that are full of anthers. They flower far into November and brighten up lifeless and gloomy spots.

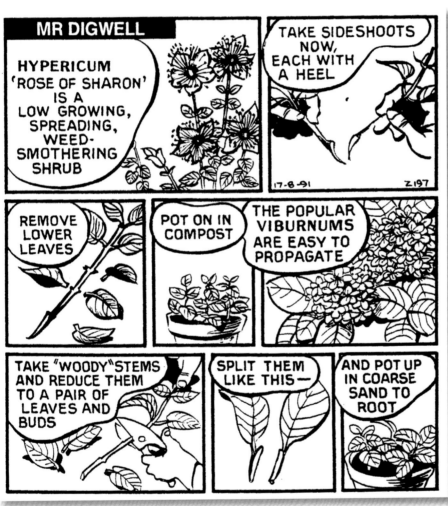

The plant has long been used in folk treatments, particularly for depression, but in the garden it is incomparable. Once it has started flowering it doesn't stop until the frosts come, and sometimes not even then.

Prune them in April, certainly not as late as May. You are restricting the size of the plant and opening it a little so branches don't touch and the wind can circulate. However, you can prune close to the ground and it will regain its height. Where they have formed a lot of ground cover I have seen them being cut to within a couple of centimetres of the ground with a large strimmer, only to see them a metre high in the summer, full of flowers.

Match them in a shrubbery with spirea; with good pruning they can both achieve a nice dome shape and the different forms of flowers will create an interesting contrast.

POLYANTHUS

Polyanthus

This flower appeared some three to four hundred years ago as a natural cross between two primulas: the cowslip and the primrose. It has since become a real favourite in the UK – because you can grow this plant on an iceberg it will cope with anything the British weather can do.

It is remarkable that these plants can be grown from seed at all, and very small seeds at that. It takes time and warmth to get them off – wait a month before beginning to worry about them.

Pop them in a cool greenhouse, unless you have a cold frame, and let them overwinter in comfort. Plant them out in April and let them grow for a year before expecting them to flower.

They flower according to the severity of the weather – a harsh one means later flowering.

Keep them weed free and give them a little mulch of well rotted manure and you will have a great display for many years.

Prickly pears

The Optunia, otherwise known as the prickly pear or paddle cactus, is great fun to grow indoors. The techniques described in the cartoon work well with many cacti, and all you need is some compost and a pair of gloves.

You don't actually need water to get this going: it has enough of its own. But then a little splash in the compost does encourage the cuttings to root.

Use the same technique with aloe vera, of which I have hundreds around the house. A slice of aloe on the hands when you have been gardening – wash them first – will leave them feeling refreshed and your skin super soft.

Aloe really is a great plant for helping the skin to heal, and can be used on minor burns, after you have held the burn under cold water.

Vegetable reminders

There are so many jobs to do at this time of the year that sometimes we forget what seem to be the little things, but it would be no small thing if we run short of produce – that would be a complete disaster – so here are a few vegetables that need to be sown and planted along with all the other August jobs.

Winter radish

You can sow these in any way, place or time. Radishes can take up any old corner of the plot, or be grown in containers anywhere. When the tomatoes are finished in the greenhouse I always sow some radish in one of the growbags.

For winter the smaller round types are the best, giving a refreshing peppery bite.

Beans

Runner beans dry up fantastically in the pod and consequently will store easily in a jar. They will last even longer if you put some uncooked rice at the bottom of the jar to remove any moisture. The beans should be fine for next year if kept cool. Don't forget to put a good label on the jar, saying what variety, when they were collected and maybe a note about how they grew.

Don't keep on using last year's seeds – take a break every couple of years to bring new stock to your garden.

Spinach

This is a brilliant leafy vegetable that lost some of its appeal because people just boiled it, and it fell into a green mash. But these days it is having a resurgence as an ingredient in stews and curries. It always was used in this way, we just didn't notice.

It is prey to the same attacks as most leaves – aphids, biting insects and so on, but as it is grown in the winter it has few if any real problems. Spinach is quite a hungry plant and prefers a lot of compost in the soil. Be careful not to overfeed it: the leaves can become dangerously high in nitrates as a result.

When the bad weather comes put a cloche over the plants so they can be kept warm and protected from the battering wind and rain.

Swiss chard

These overwinter quite well and are almost like spinach in the way you deal with them. Keep them weed free and cloche as necessary, more to get really perfect leaves than for any other reason.

September

One minute the summer was here and all of a sudden, with the aroma of rising mists and damp soils, the world is facing the other way and it is September! Actually, when you consider the enormous forces at work – that the gravity of the sun is dragging us around so we start our journey across the other side of the solar system – the changes on the planet are quite gentle.

For me autumn starts when the swallows go home, the deadheading stops working, the lawn doesn't grow so quickly and there is a lot of condensation on the windows of the house, the greenhouse and the cold frames.

Truth be told, you can wax lyrical about the end of the summer, but only from afar. You see, in September you are far too busy to notice these things. There is the harvest to start getting in.

There is also the worry about ripening this and bottling that and deciding if we should have a clamp this year or just give stuff away. Before you know it the summer returns – the Indian variety – and the garden starts to think it's August once again.

Week by week

If there is one thing you do in September it is make sure you have a watertight and vermin proof shed or place to store your crops. Otherwise the precious produce will not last until the end of November.

Week 1

Plant out bulbs for next spring, leaving tulips until late October

Feed lawns with autumn feed

Cut out foliage from tomato plants to encourage good fruit

Harvest grapes

Week 2

Earth up celery, leaving a small amount of foliage

Deadhead roses and the last of the summer flowers

Use green waste in the compost bin, turning it over to aerate

Water shrubs

Week 3

Scarify the lawn to remove debris

Harvest your apples

Clean out the greenhouse after tomatoes have finished

Sow spring flowering plants in the greenhouse

Week 4

Cut down hydrangeas to a healthy pair of leaves

Plant new trees, such as apple, cherry or pear

Tidy up the garden for winter, composting green waste

Seed the lawn and water generously

Digwell garden basics

September is a good time to come into gardening because in a way things are getting easier. And they are also getting clearer – what I mean is, you can actually see the shape of the garden and work out what you want to do with it.

Soil

People new to gardening see all there is to do and learn and it seems to be insurmountable, a bit like learning a foreign language. But if you start with the basics, and get them right, you can't go far wrong.

You cannot get more basic than soil. The first test I would do is a moisture test. All you need to do is to take a handful of soil and squeeze it. If moisture comes out, it's too wet. If it sticks together it's still too wet. If it just starts to fall apart when you open your hand, it is just right.

Too wet and you might need to look at your drainage.

Then look for weeds growing on your soil. Chickweed shows it is very fertile. Perennial weeds, like dock and mare's tail show the ground has been left alone for a long time. Sedges confirm the soil is wet.

What do you want your garden to do?

There are lots of designs for gardens, some in this book, and I don't want to go into them now. But you do need to ask yourself some questions.

What do you want the garden to do?

Who is going to actually use the garden, and what will they need – include the pets in this too!

What kind of garden do you need? Flowers, herb, wildlife, food?

What kinds of plants do you actually like?

Add to this the need for security, and you will have a pretty long list of things to do.

Security for gardens is important because it is your first line of defence, and people do steal from gardens. There are many things you can do, including having good, thick, prickly hedges of blackthorn, mahonia or pyracantha.

Then get a good, strong, lockable gate and security lights.

Path areas with shale or pea shingle, so that you cannot get to the grass or any other surface without walking on them – they make a noise and that puts undesirables off.

Planting in the garden

The variety of plants on the planet is astounding. So much so that even experts are baffled about which plant goes where in the great scheme of things.

You need to include all of these types of plants in your garden, and my advice is to start with just a few and build up slowly. Getting to know just a few plants is better than buying lots and not even remembering their names.

Step back and draw a plan, which contains not only the position of the plants you want, but how high they grow. Careful examination of seed catalogues will help in this regard.

One of the good things about starting a garden in September is the winter period is not that far away. You can therefore plant bare-rooted shrubs and trees, and if they don't look quite right, with care, you can move them.

Planting shrubs

Shrubs are the cornerstone of the garden. They make an overall shape but, as they basically never change, you need to like what you plant.

You might need to work at the soil before you plant, for example, if you want to grow rhododendrons and azaleas, you need to have ericaceous, or acidic, compost. This might be a dramatic change – especially if you live on a lime soil. So, again, it is important to check your soil.

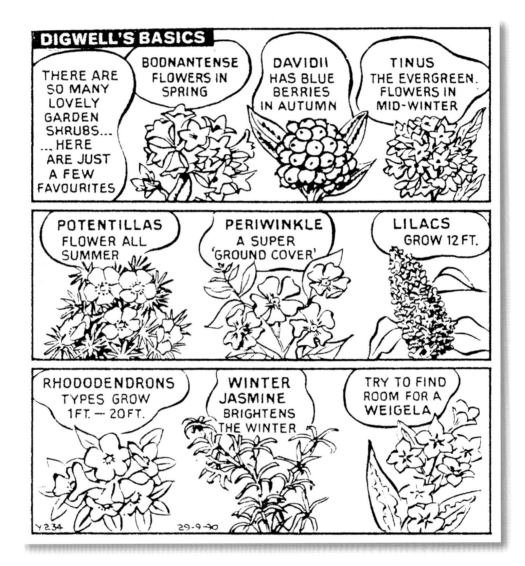

Some of the most wonderful shrubs are so easy to keep. Buddleia is so easy to grow you find huge specimens on the top of derelict buildings. If you cut it back hard every autumn it will come back each summer, and you will avoid leggy stems.

I always say it is better to avoid ground cover plants, because at some time you are going to want to remove them. Only use such plants if you are sure they will be in place for many years.

New gardeners should choose azaleas over rhododendrons because they tend to be more compact and are therefore easier to deal with than a plant that will become much higher than you think.

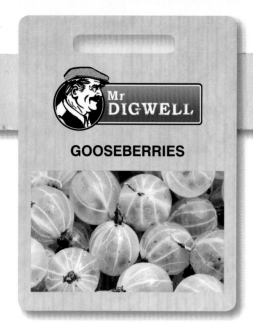

GOOSEBERRIES

Gooseberries are a funny fruit: you either love them or hate them. They are reasonably easy to grow so long as you remember that they are full of sugar and moisture, and consequently they fall prey to fungal attack.

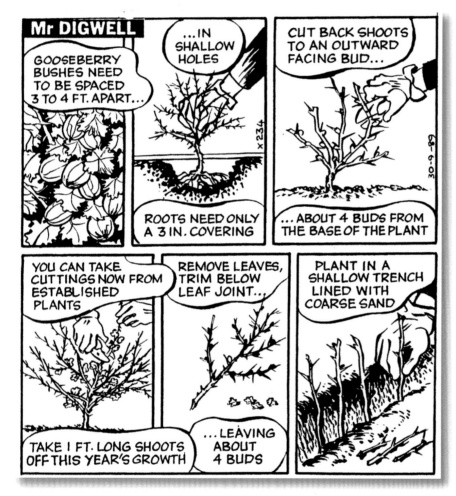

Mr DIGWELL

GOOSEBERRY BUSHES NEED TO BE SPACED 3 TO 4 FT. APART...

...IN SHALLOW HOLES

ROOTS NEED ONLY A 3 IN. COVERING

CUT BACK SHOOTS TO AN OUTWARD FACING BUD...

...ABOUT 4 BUDS FROM THE BASE OF THE PLANT

YOU CAN TAKE CUTTINGS NOW FROM ESTABLISHED PLANTS

TAKE 1 FT. LONG SHOOTS OFF THIS YEAR'S GROWTH

REMOVE LEAVES, TRIM BELOW LEAF JOINT...

...LEAVING ABOUT 4 BUDS

PLANT IN A SHALLOW TRENCH LINED WITH COARSE SAND

There are many types, some give small, very sweet fruits, others give tart large ones. You can get mildew resistant ones, too.

Prune the bushes in the winter, cutting last year's growth to two buds. Then, minding the spines, you can cut out all the branches that point to the centre of the bush. Make a goblet shape, which will allow for easier picking of the fruit and air to circulate.

You can spray with Bordeaux Mixture against fungal infection – it mostly works fine, but doesn't guarantee success. Feed with a mulch of well rotted manure in the spring. An early summer top dressing of organic fertilizer also helps.

When you water, don't splash it all over the plant but try to keep the leaves and fruit as dry as possible.

Watch out for sawfly – it will eat all your leaves in one go. If it does, prune the plant back hard and it will recover.

LILIES

Lilies

The lily family is one of the most prolific in the garden, and many of the beautiful flowers we have belong to that category. They almost invariably have trumpet-like flowers made of a number of petals with vivid colours – almost every colour under the sun.

You buy lily bulbs, made of lots of swollen leaves sometimes referred to as "scales". These will individually grow into new plants and, as the plants get old after a few years, the scales will be fatter and easier to handle.

You can get some enormous and stunningly beautiful lilies – 'Triumphator' is one of my favourites and is one of the Asiatic types.

Being native to most of the northern hemisphere they are categorized into a number of groups: Asiatic ones bearing

big, ginger-smelling flowers; American lilies, which are very tall and divide by rhizomes; longifolium types, used for cut flowers, and many other hybrids besides.

They are quite hungry plants and like a rich compost to grow in. They are just as at home in containers as they are in borders, and prefer full sun.

Dividing lilies

If you buy a lily bulb and plant it in a 30cm pot, at the end of the first year's growth you should remove the stalk when the leaves are turning. Give the pot a dressing of organic fertilizer and set it in a cool, preferably frost-free place. The following year you will get possibly two lilies, and this will increase year on year. After about three years, empty the pot onto a sheet of newspaper and remove the bulbs. You will find more than one. You can pot these on singly.

If you are building a herbaceous border, you will do well with lilies – mix them with equally delicate and beautiful plants – dahlias, alliums, agapanthus. One of lilies' most beautiful attributes is the delicate anthers and stamens that fall out of the flower like antennae.

QUICK TIP: *Look out for the lily beetle, nibbling both leaves and flowers. You can catch him on the plant as he is bright red, but if he falls off, you won't be able to see him – he is black underneath!*

Ripening tomatoes

One of the problems of a cool wet summer is the mountains of tomatoes you have to try to ripen.

GREEN TOMATOES

GOSH! I'LL NEVER RIPEN ALL THESE!

AH! EASIEST WAY'S TO REMOVE THE STAKES AND LAY THE **PLANTS** DOWN ON DRY PEAT OR CUT-UP STRAW

COVER WITH WELL-VENTILATED CLOCHES

BUT KEEP THE GLASS CLEAN—THEY'LL WANT ALL THE LIGHT POSSIBLE

IF YOU'VE A GREENHOUSE, LAY THE FRUIT ON DRY STRAW ON THE STAGING— (**NOT** TOUCHING!)

OR HANG THE WHOLE TRUSSES IN A WARM, SUNNY PLACE

OF COURSE, THERE'S THE OLD DODGE OF STORING THEM IN A DRAWER WRAPPED IN TISSUE PAPER OR NEWSPAPER

BUT SEE THAT THE DRAWER'S **NOT** AIR-TIGHT, AND LOOK 'EM OVER CAREFULLY NOW AND THEN

One of the amazing things about studying plants is what remarkable things plants can achieve with only five hormones. And, more than that, one of these hormones is a gas! Ethylene gas is a hormone, and we have known of its effects for a long time. In Victorian times, when they put gas street lamps in place, a large number of trees died and no one knew why. In fact, ethylene, found in small amounts in town gas, was killing the trees. Nearly all town plants from that time on were those who could tolerate ethylene gas!

Ethylene is in charge of ripening and aging the plant (senescence). So, if you put unripe tomatoes in a drawer, and then put a ripe banana in a sock beside them, the toms will be ripe in a week.

Don't stop making green tomato chutney though, it's delicious!

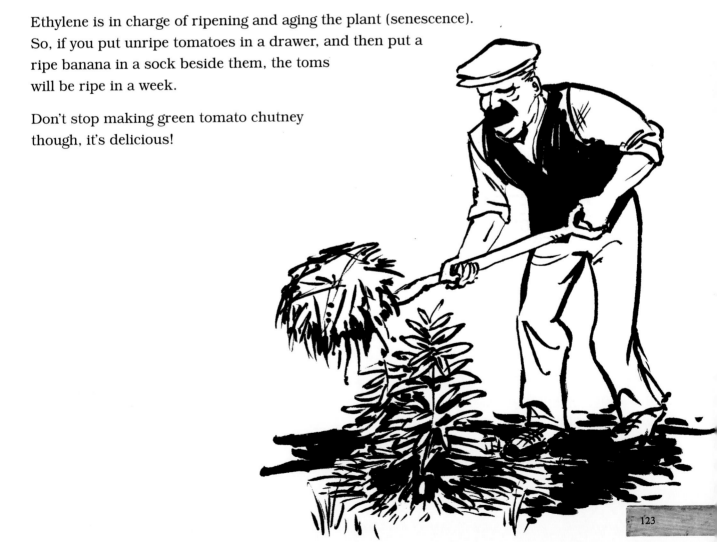

Lawn MOT

We have looked at lawns a lot in this book – but in September it is time to go to town and really get it right. Set aside a few days for this because it's a big job – but the lawn will be better for it.

You need a good grass rake for this job – a garden rake won't do. Some people use an attachment on their rotavator but I still prefer to use the rake – it gives me a good workout. You need to scratch all the dead grass out of the lawn – you'll get a lot of it too!

Dead grass acts like a sponge, collecting water, and weeds and moss will grow in it, so it has to be removed.

Removing moss

If you have a mossy lawn, remove the moss with a rake and chop up the soil with a hoe. Then you can reseed that spot. Hopefully it won't be much – normally it is about the size of a saucer. If the lawn is very patchy and mossy, think about drainage. Large patches of moss mean that the lawn will need to be overseeded.

I try not to use moss killer, but have had great success with weed and feed applications in the past.

Aeration

I have to say that the only way for doing this job properly remains the garden fork. If you must use a machine, make sure it makes big holes at least the equivalent of a centimetre in diameter! Aeration does what it says – gets air to the roots – and you need to make good-sized holes every 20cm or so around the lawn. This is a sweaty job!

Top dressing

Experts recently did some work on the bowling green that Captain Drake played on at the time of the Armada. When dug up, it showed lines all through as layer upon layer of top dressing was applied every year. I wonder if the grass is still the same one as that which was sown all those years ago?

Top dressing is made from loam and fertilizer. The soil has been riddled (passed through a garden sieve) and then sprinkled over the grass. I used to use the back of a garden rake to spread it around – about a third of a bucket per square metre – but I now use a stiff brush, lightly so I don't hurt the grass. If I have reseeded parts of the lawn, I don't top dress those areas this time.

QUICK TIP: *The best thing for growing grass is water – so if September is dry, give it a good soaking every day.*

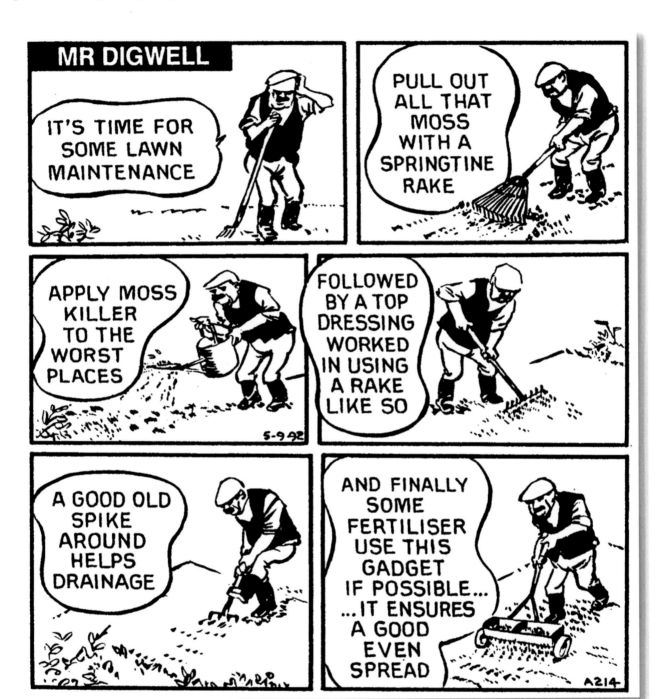

When I used to run a football pitch, the fire brigade used to come and water the grass for us!

LAVENDER

Lavender

We have a love affair with lavender: it is so lovely in many ways. The look of the plant is spectacular and you cannot fail to notice the aroma! But more than this, lavender is so very useful. As well as having a wonderful scent, it is a brilliant antiseptic.

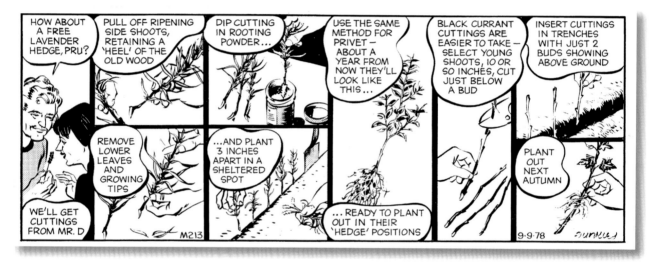

Lavender likes to grow in a sandy soil. Any hint of heaviness and it recoils. It grows well in large containers, which I fill with ⅓ sand, ⅓ loam and ⅓ good quality compost.

Plant in this mixture and then give a coating of pea shingle on the top, which not only looks good, but helps with drainage.

It is the retention of water at the roots of lavender that causes root rot – a fungal infection – so don't mulch the plant and don't overwater it. Feed with an application of organic liquid feed in the spring, and another in the summer.

Avoid using mulches of any kind, they keep the soil moist that encourages the spore that will produce root rot.

Take the flowers as you need them: this is a good way of pruning the plant and the more you take the more the plant produce. Also, give lavender a good trim in spring. Reduce branches by ½, which will encourage new growth, stopping the plant from becoming too woody.

Planting trees

This is one time where the gardener needs to see the bigger picture. Trees might look pretty in a bag in the garden centre, but in three years' time things might be quite different.

At one time we all went mad growing leylandii conifers, and 20 years later they are bigger than our homes and cut out the light. They have been banned in many places. The problem is they grow so quickly, so if you miss a year's pruning you simply can't reach them and it's easy to just give up on them.

Fit the tree to your circumstances, not the other way round, and if you want a hedge for privacy go for blackthorn, hawthorn and other medium height plants that have big spines.

When you plant your tree, dig a big hole! At least twice as deep and wide as the root ball, and give the bottom a good 20cm layer of well rotted manure or compost. Remember to support the tree as it is vulnerable to the wind for at least a year. It might not fall over, but it will rock and this will damage the roots.

Autumn to Winter

Whether we have a mild or a long, snow-covered and frost-filled winter, there's always a job to keep us busy and occupied, safe in the knowledge that soon enough, the snow will be gone and up will pop the snowdrops as heralds of spring. A roaring fire and a good stew will combat the chills from a day spent working outside, and though everything in the garden seems dead at the moment, before you know it the plants will be out again and the whole cycle will begin all over again.

Nothing is lost in each season. It is a mistake that many new to gardening think that winter is simply a closed season, when everything is either asleep or dead. There is lots going on, and I can tell you that one of a gardener's best friends is frost. Of course, frost can destroy tender plants, so it's important to protect what you have to avoid losing them. But many of our pests and disease organisms are killed off in a good hard frost, so rather than worrying about all that bad weather, welcome the benefits the winter brings to our garden.

In this section

October

This is a month of preparation and boy do we need it! The garden can resemble a building site, dissected and pulled apart. It is nice to watch the birds pick at the grubs in the turned soil and realize this is a great way of cleaning your garden from pests for the next year.

October is a very sociable month, especially on the allotment. It is a time when you can get all kinds of freebies, from rhubarb crowns that have been dug up and divided to corms and bulbs of all kinds. It pays to be a friendly gardener: you never know what's coming your way.

There are a lot of plants that need to be sown this month too. Beans, sweet peas indoors and, of course, garlic. This is also the time to hunt down a supplier of paraffin – all the old shops are disappearing. The last shop that sold me heating fuel for my garden heaters was bulldozed, and is now a supermarket. Take the time to check all your heaters and ventilators. The last thing you want is to have nothing to combat a sharp frost.

Week by week

October is a month of apples, pears, muck and magic. There are loads of salads you can sow, but work on the greenhouse is important as well. Outside, your beds need clearing and the soil preparing for next year in order to get the best results when we start the gardening process all over again.

Week 1

Rake the lawn for fallen leaves, and compost

Bring in houseplants that have been outside for the summer

Cut back geraniums

Sow sweet peas in pots in the greenhouse

Week 2

Harvest pumpkins and squash

Harvest apples that were not ready in September

Cut off foliage from maincrop potatoes and compost the green waste

Harvest beans

Week 3

Harvest and store carrots in sand

Remove tomatoes from vines and ripen indoors

Fertilize vacant spots on the surface and dig in

Turn compost bins to aid decomposition

Week 4

Harvest maincrop potatoes

Plant garlic

Remove dead leaves of strawberry plants and any rotting berries

Prune fruit bushes and plant new canes

ALLIUMS

Alliums

Alliums make a fantastic impact on even the smallest of gardens, and can be an integral part of a herbaceous border or simply grown on their own in pots. Don't let their close relationship to onions and garlic put you off – there'll be no strong smells on your patio!

Ornamental alliums can be bought as bulbs and will grow to up to four feet high, depending on the variety. They frequently produce a large ball of flowers that looks like a little firework explosion, and will give you a fantastic show all summer long.

Bulbs should be planted outside in early autumn, as with most spring flowering bulbs, in a bed you've prepared with fertilizer. Alliums do well in pots too, though for the larger varieties, make sure it's a deep one. Throw some grit into the bottom for drainage and use a multipurpose compost for best results.

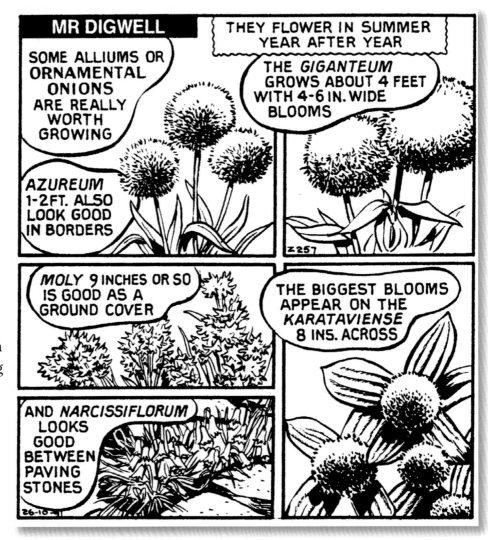

MR DIGWELL

SOME ALLIUMS OR ORNAMENTAL ONIONS ARE REALLY WORTH GROWING

AZUREUM 1-2FT. ALSO LOOK GOOD IN BORDERS

THEY FLOWER IN SUMMER YEAR AFTER YEAR

THE *GIGANTEUM* GROWS ABOUT 4 FEET WITH 4-6 IN. WIDE BLOOMS

MOLY 9 INCHES OR SO IS GOOD AS A GROUND COVER

THE BIGGEST BLOOMS APPEAR ON THE *KARATAVIENSE* 8 INS. ACROSS

AND *NARCISSIFLORUM* LOOKS GOOD BETWEEN PAVING STONES

The bulbs will produce offsets next year, and can be easily divided to improve your show the year after. Don't cut the foliage down when the flowers have faded, as the seed pods look fantastic for weeks. It is best to leave them to die back naturally, as then the bulb will have soaked up as much of the energy through the foliage as possible, making them that bit better for next year.

Garlic

GARLIC

Garlic is one of our culinary wonders and not only tastes fantastic but is really good for your health. It helps stave off colds and flu and what surprises many people is just how easy this tasty plant is to grow – and it's not just the French who can do it!

Garlic is best grown from new bulbs, so don't save bulbs at the end of the season as your crop will not be at its best. The segments, or corms, can be individually planted, though don't use bulbs bought from a supermarket, as they are usually shipped in from the Mediterranean and may not be suited to the UK climate. Garlic from the garden centre will give you the best results.

Plant the bulbs in late autumn or early winter, as garlic is better if the frost gets to them. You will need beds or pots of well-draining soil. Add some sand if you need extra drainage, and don't mulch them as this will rot the bulbs. Keep up with the weeding as they can get overrun, being smaller plants.

Garlic leaves are a lovely addition to salads, though your bulbs are not ready until the foliage has turned yellow. Lift them carefully with a hand fork and leave them to dry out like onions, to form a papery skin.

You may find the birds try and pull the plants up but a netting layer should solve this problem.

Spring and summer bulbs

Naturalizing bulbs into a lawn is nothing new – we are recreating the woodland edge, and most of these plants will be fine in anything from semi-shade to full sun.

Anemone

These are daisy-like flowers that bloom every month of the year in their different varieties. They are sold as bulbs and they need very little attention. They're a great plant for every garden.

Muscari

Grape hyacinths are super little plants. They pop out of the soil year after year with long, bent over leaves and flower stalks bearing little bell-shaped flowers. They are best grown in clumps so the effects are compounded.

Dwarf iris

If there is a plant you should grow it's this one! It doesn't particularly need soil that is wet – they do well in almost anything except clay.

Scilla

This is also known as the Siberian squill, and this gives you an idea of its hardiness. Plant a few in the border's edge or the lawn and it will naturally increase itself until you have a clump. In fact it does this so naturally you would have thought it was a master gardener! An extract of the bulb is used in cough medicine.

Garden frame and hot bed

Sometimes the old-fashioned ways are still the best and, especially if you have a small garden, a cold frame is a great idea. I wonder if you have any idea why it is called a cold frame?

Hot and cold

The cold frame is named because it is unheated, but you can make a simple heated frame, which would be called a hot frame. You can also have a hot bed.

Dig a hole at least 60cm deep and put the soil somewhere convenient, for example, on other beds. Then half fill this hole with horse manure – raw horse manure. Fill it to the top with compost and put the frame over that. As the manure rots it gives off heat, and this will permeate the compost. The horse manure will take a month to get going and then another month to start to slowly cool.

Building one now, you will be able to plant in the compost in January.

However, you don't need horse manure – try vegetable waste from the kitchen it works just as well. If you use cow manure it gets really hot, and you can put plants in pots and containers on the compost – but don't plant in it.

Double digging

This is an old-fashioned trick that really improves the nature of your soil and is not often done these days. It is a way of increasing the value of your subsoil while not ruining the overall structure.

You have to be used to digging. Make sure you only dig within your capabilities and be realistic with yourself. As soon as you get backache, stop! Ten minutes a day for a week will turn into 20 minutes a day soon enough, so don't overdo it.

You are taking out soil two spades deep and setting aside the soil from the first trench. Half fill the first trench with compost or well rotted manure, and then dig the second trench. Use some of the soil from the second trench to cover the first, and repeat the compost filling. Make your way in this manner down the bed, and when you have finished spread the rest of the soil from the first trench evenly over the bed.

While you are at it you can take out any perennial weeds you find too!

Care for winter veg

You know, it's hardly frost that bothers vegetables because we are always watching for it and in most cases make the right preparations. It's constant battering from wind and rain that gets to them and ruins what would have been a promising crop.

Sowing anything outside at this time of year is always a bit hit and miss but try to cover the ground with a cloche so the plants make use of whatever warmth there is and they are hidden from drying winds.

Use the draw hoe to pack soil around any plants that might be blown about by the wind – the extra support will be very useful and you can always wash the soil off when you need to.

Autumn broad beans are possibly the only ones not to be bothered by the rain – but pop some old twigs in place for support and to dissipate the wind. Better still, cover them with horticultural fleece.

November

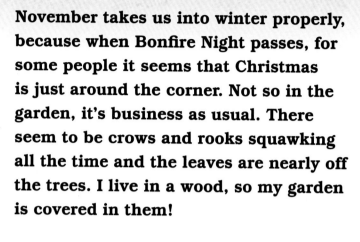

November takes us into winter properly, because when Bonfire Night passes, for some people it seems that Christmas is just around the corner. Not so in the garden, it's business as usual. There seem to be crows and rooks squawking all the time and the leaves are nearly off the trees. I live in a wood, so my garden is covered in them!

It is a good time for learning something new. When I went to France last year in December I was amazed how cold it was! I then started to think about all those vines, freezing to death, compared to mine in a cool greenhouse. The penny dropped – vines actually are very hardy, it's the grapes that need sun and warmth!

So why not make a wire frame fence to support some vines? Set them now and leave them for a couple of weeks before you put vines against them – you can then tighten the wires without the plants getting in the way.

Week by week

For the first time in the year the world takes on a different aspect, as leaves are finally cleared away from trees. You can see parts of the garden that, perhaps, you could not see before. This is an ideal opportunity to think hard about your garden design, especially to see if it is appropriate for the autumn. Of course, some gardens are at their best when the leaves change colour, and it is well worth planting a Japanese maple somewhere – just for the russets they bring to the landscape.

Week 1

Sweep up leaves and compost

Mulch the soil to protect it over winter

Plant tulips

Protect plants prone to frost with cloches or bubble wrap

Week 2

Keep the mower, spade and tools in good order by cleaning blades and oiling

Check roses for black spot and burn the leaves. Do not compost

Dig over empty beds

Sow hardy pea varieties in pots or trays

Week 3

Net over brassicas to keep off birds

Plant new canes of fruit bushes, such as raspberries and blackberries

Support young trees with stakes

Prune apple and pear trees

Week 4

Transplant any shrubs or trees that need moving

Clear away fallen branches and leaves

Mulch around frost-prone plants

Planning your borders

Late autumn is when the thump of seed catalogues landing on the doormat signifies it's time to get planning next year's borders. You can't move for brochures falling out of magazines, all because they know now is the right time to order your stock for next year.

Most gardens, whether large or small, benefit from a well-planned border that can give you a good show all summer long. Whatever the shape of your bed, the main rule is to place the tallest plants at the back and smallest at the front. This will give depth to the bed, making your space look bigger and your garden all the better.

If you have an island bed, place your tallest plants, such as alliums or helianthus, in the centre of the island, with the shorter around the edge.

You really can go to town with your borders, but try to keep an overall theme for best results through colours, textures or shapes. Interspersing cultivars with a packet of wild flowers will give you a more natural, cottage feel.

Before you begin, make sure your beds are prepared for your show by digging in manure and keeping the bed as weed free as possible. It is all very well to plan the structure and colour of your bed, but if the ground is not adequate to house your plants the border will not achieve its potential.

Pruning apple trees

This is another plea! Around the country there used to be a variety of apple for every county, often five or six! Now they are languishing as forgotten old trees in gardens and allotments. These apple trees are being cut down and possibly lost forever. So, if you have an old apple tree, prune it and see if you can get it back into production.

.

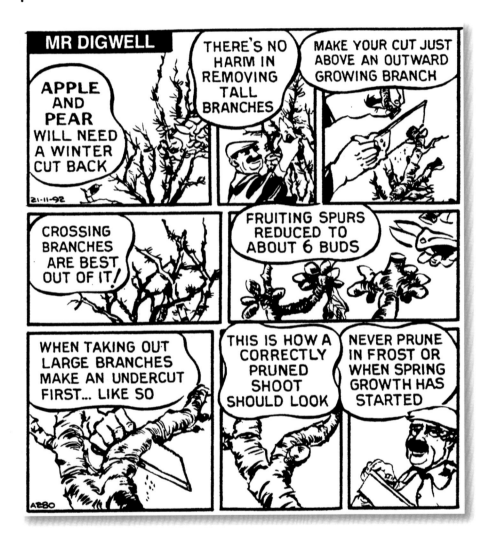

Generally apples and pears can be treated in the same way. Reduce branches by a third of their length, cut out crossing branches and try to get them to grow horizontally rather than vertically.

The undercut is a really useful technique – when you are cutting a branch off the weight of the branch doesn't tear the bark or the wood as it falls off and you get a clean cut.

If you like you can paint the cut surface with wound paint to keep it free from infection.

Keep the prunings: apple wood is great for smoking fish!

Planting berries

This method applies to most berries: blackberries, currants, and everything where you have to prune hard back after planting.

Plants that shed their leaves can be more or less said to be under a general anaesthetic, and the basic idea is you give the plant a head start as soon as it wakes up. It will be a bit groggy at first, and it will suffer setbacks if the weather nips its growth, but the home we have placed it in should see it through.

First of all make sure the hole isn't shaded – these plants like full sun. Make the hole plenty big enough for the roots and fill the bottom with good compost and a spade of organic fertilizer. If you are on a clay soil make your hole an additional 15cm deeper, and fill that with organic fertilizer to act as an under blanket to keep it warm.

Drive the stake in and then put the plant in – spreading the roots. Fill in the hole, press the soil down hard and tie the plant to the stake. Then cut the stems to about 20cm. Job done.

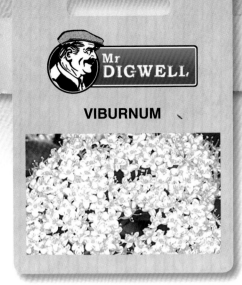

VIBURNUM

Viburnum

Viburnum is a great plant, well worth its place in any garden. Its dark green foliage makes great contrast to the drabness of the winter garden, and its flowers make a change from other super plants such as skimmia. The various varieties give quite different flowers and they also flower at different times of the year.

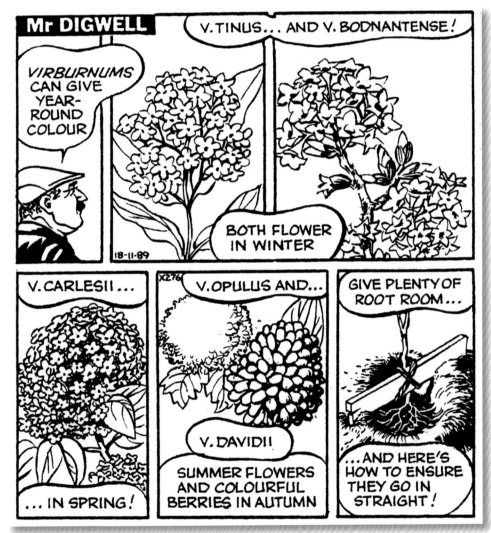

From the medieval-sounding guelder rose with its large flowers, almost like a hydrangea, to the tiny flowered *V. davidii*, these plants have much variety. And when the flowers are gone, the berries, often bright shiny and red, continue the interest. Sometimes these plants bear flowers in clusters, making them look sparse, sometimes they are simply huge and full.

Viburnum also hybridizes well, giving a wonderful fragrance. A cross of *V. grandiflorum* and species *V. farrer* is simply full of nose – you can smell it across the garden.

A prune after flowering is advisable and generally these plants respond well to a summer feed.

Growing fruit in pots

If all you have is a patio you can still grow a lot of fruit, and anything else for that matter, in pots and containers. I knew a lady once who had over 60 pots with trees of all kinds in a space no bigger than a living room. She had to move them out of the way to get to the one she was working on!

Plants do grow in containers very well, even big ones, but there are some rules you have to stick to before you go ahead!

Plants in containers run out of water easily, and so you have to water them daily – even if it is pouring down.

Then, with all this watering they run out of nutrients easily. This is because the water simply washes it away. You therefore have to replace these nutrients. Matters are helped by using slow release fertilizer pellets, but with every other watering you need to add a little soluble fertilizer – not necessarily a full whack – just a little.

Then, as the plant grows you need to repot it and, for those that have been pruned, replace the compost they are growing in.

Growing in pots is a great way of giving some fruit trees exactly the conditions they need, and has been done for years. Two hundred years ago wealthy houses would treat oranges in just this way.

Growing exotics

We all buy fruits from all over the world in supermarkets and it has long been a fun pastime to see if you can grow from the seeds we would otherwise throw away.

Obviously we can grow oranges, apples and olives (when fresh) quite easily. It is just a case of waiting for them to germinate. I have a friend with an olive tree he swears he sowed himself, and it does bear fruit.

Apricot stones will grow, but it takes years for them to come to anything.

Pineapples are easy and fun. Peel back the leaves and you will find little bracts, which you pop in compost. These will grow – but not flower.

But there are some plants from the supermarket from which you can get a good crop. Sweet potatoes are just one. Cut them up into pieces that each have a bud and plant them in May. They will come up and grow just like potatoes – and you will get a great crop of tubers by the end of the summer.

And one other tip – those so-called living herbs. They are almost always tasteless, but if you pop them out of the container they come in and into some compost they will soon come on and do well – and taste much better too!

December

The coats are out, the scarves are on and you can see clouds of white breath on the air as the winter gardener puffs and pants to get things ready for spring. Though it may seem as if there's little to do during these months, the frosts and the snow can give you extra work on top of the pruning, tidying and turning of the soil that needs to be done. Heavy snowfall can really cause havoc with large trees, with their branches breaking under the weight.

December is the time to decide on what you are going to plant next year. Seed and bulb catalogues will be arriving on the doormat or falling out of magazines, so a bit of early planning will allow you to get the cheapest prices and set things in motion to give you the best results next year. A good, clean greenhouse will give you a great home for seedlings that need starting off in the winter.

The plants may not be full of life but the winter garden is always full of beauty, with frost-covered umbels or ice-blue frost-covered lawns. To add a splash of colour I usually plant a few pansies that give a happy glimpse of something alive here and there.

Week by week

Back in the autumn I put a cloche where the snowdrops and lily of the valley were growing, warming the soil enough to hopefully bring them on. It doesn't always work, but it's nice to get a white Christmas in flower form. It's busy in the greenhouse, too, potting up all those pressies in nice gift pots. I always wrap them on Christmas Eve, and if there is any time left I sow my onions.

Week 1

Clear flower borders of leaves and debris

If it has snowed, clear as much as possible from branches to prevent them becoming too heavy

Dig out annuals, turning over the soil

Plant trees and shrubs before snowfall

Week 2

Prune outdoor vines

Plant pansies in pots for winter colour

Take cuttings of roses

Check on stored crops, such as potatoes or carrots, for mould and rot

Week 3

Water evergreens and shrubs that are sheltered

Check ties on stakes for young trees

Add protection for camellias, azaleas and rhododendrons

Mulch strawberries with straw

Week 4

Top dress fruit trees with manure

Turn the compost heap

Check greenhouse plants and use a heater if temperatures drop

Bring all tender plants under cover (in greenhouse, cold frame and so on)

Christmas holly

There is nothing more festive than bright red berries against spiky emerald leaves. A wreath of holly on the door at Christmas has more impact than hundreds of pounds' worth of bought decorations, and will make a fantastic all-year-round addition to the garden.

As most people who read books about teenage wizards will know, holly is a tree and should be treated as such. It is native to Britain and is evergreen, growing up to around 10 metres if not checked. Prune holly bushes carefully with secateurs, not hedge trimmers, as this will give you the best results and avoid sharp leaves flying off and hitting you in the eye!

Holly is dioecious (or either male or female) so you

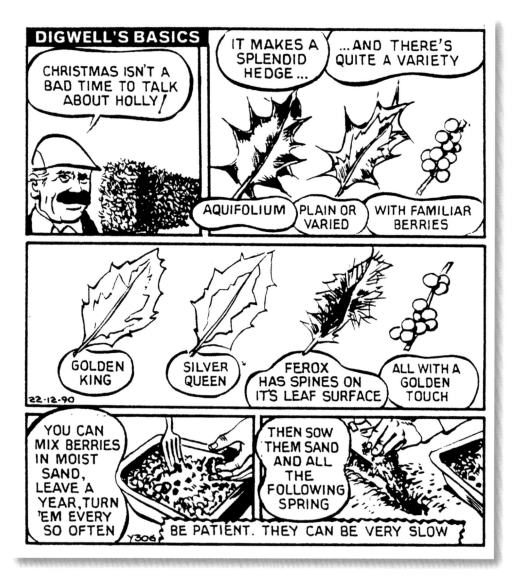

will not get berries in every case. Fertilized female flowers develop into those lovely shiny red berries, which are initially green but ripen up to that characteristic scarlet by Christmas. However, trees will not begin to flower until the tree is about 20 years old, so do not expect berries in new plants.

Holly makes a good alternative to privets in hedges, with the additional benefit of the spiky leaves deterring trespassers trying to get through! It will take a while to achieve it, but the shiny leaves will give you a lifetime's pleasure once they are in place.

Mistletoe

This amazing plant is having a resurgence in one way and a depression in another. The depression is because it is becoming rarer each year. Where I used to live there were hundreds of them in apple orchards all over the south-west. Now there are not so many, and where I live now, I have only seen one plant. On the other hand, the plant is in the public eye once again because a substance found inside has been found to cure some kinds of cancer.

The host of choice for this semi-parasitic plant is the apple, but it will grow on others. It is easy to sow the seeds but not so easy to see them germinate. What the books don't tell you is the best way to get the seed to take – after you have cut into the apple branch and placed the seed inside – is to slap a handful of well rotted manure on it and rub it in.

I expect the plant pathologists amongst us will be mortified at such treatment – but it works well.

Azaleas

Azaleas are stunning flowering shrubs and are found as both indoor and outdoor varieties – they generally come from the Far East and New Zealand. In Chinese culture they are known as "the thinking of home bush". They need acidic soil and therefore have to be planted in ericaceous compost.

Azaleas sold as pot plants for Christmas are unlikely to flower again next Christmas – a lot of work has gone into making them flower for the Christmas market that we will be unable to repeat at home. The best way to keep them going is to water, water, water. Don't let them dry out at all. You can give them a little house plant fertilizer if you will, but the water is the most important thing. You can pot them on or take cuttings, but remember the ericaceous compost.

The hardier types go well outside and you get summer flowering. The colours of azaleas seem to be more vivid and striking year on year, and 'Palestrina' certainly gives masses of white flowers, habituated by bees. The nectar is so good, you get bumblebees asleep on them – and you can stroke them – it's a real treat.

Christmas cacti gifts

I like to give cacti as Christmas presents, but not just a single plant. It's possible to buy them relatively cheaply and then pot several different varieties of plants into unusual or interesting containers. Chances are no one else will have thought of doing this and you'll have no fear of duplicating someone else's gift.

Cacti have a number of requirements for them to become good growing specimens. They are used to living in very warm, dry conditions where there is little or no material in the soil – their only source of nutrients are the bits of rotting cacti around them.

Their soil should basically be very free draining and more or less inert. In the soil you can add pearlite, potting soil, peat, coir, pumice – all of which make good substrates for cacti.

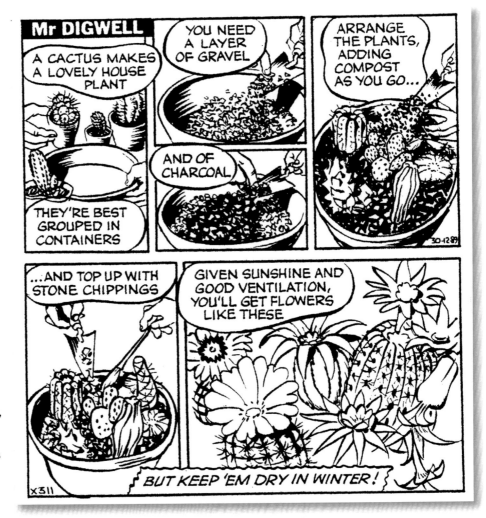

While they (mostly) live in the desert they do like to be watered in the summer. Making a Christmas present of them can be a long-term job, good watering in the summer is essential to their growth – it is during the winter they are able to survive completely without it.

When you have made your arrangement, place it on a warm windowsill, but one without a radiator beside it. The plants will need a couple of weeks to settle in before being given away.

LILY OF THE VALLEY

Lily of the valley

Who could not love this darling little plant? We seem to talk about lily of the valley a lot at Christmas, perhaps it is because it is one of the names ascribed to the infant Jesus. Some say they represent Eve's tears on being thrown out of the Garden of Eden. With plants like this about, it must have been some comfort! The other reason they are popular at this time is that, if you keep them out of the weather, they will flower at the holiday season.

The spike that bears the flowers is called an inflorescence, and in this case it sets them off perfectly.

These plants are poisonous, woodland in origin and beautiful. Along with bluebells, the rhizomes were used to glue together Elizabethan gentlemen's ruffs, which they used to wear around their necks. Lily of the valley will grow more or less anywhere if you allow them good drainage and give them a feed of fertilizer in the summer.

Ground cover

Lily of the valley will spread quite a lot and you need to take account of this in your planting. It spreads by rhizomes and grows faster than the tide comes in. I know of at least a couple of instances where they have been planted in a sunken half barrel to keep them at bay. You get excellent ground cover with lily of the valley, which looks amazing.

Some people consider them to be weeds, perhaps this is because they do need attention – you can't just leave them to their own devices. They can begin to look sad, less green and more ragged, but if you thin them out they will perk up amazingly.

Buying lily of the valley

You can buy them as rhizomes and the best time to plant them is in the winter. Just dig a scrape about 10cm deep and place them as you need them. Ask for "pips", which is the name for the rhizomes and the roots attached to them.

Early spring onions

December is onion month – you can't avoid them. Traditionally the days for sowing onions are Christmas Day and Boxing Day, but I don't know anyone that sows them then. But early spring onions are a bit of a must!

This is a method called seed forcing or etiolating. This word literally means reaching for the heavens, and that's what plants do. If you keep seeds in darkness, they behave as though they are deep in the soil and start a rush job to get to the surface. The result is a long thin seedling, which is about to die once the food in the seed is used up.

You have to keep your eye on them, and if you are as much as a day too late you can lose them. However, once they have grown, and look all yellow and insipid, place them in the light and they will colour up quickly and grow like mad. They seem never to lose this urgency to grow, and so long as you keep them in a warm greenhouse they will continue to grow quickly.

Leaf cuttings

I know at least one specialist nursery that started this off as a hobby, making cuttings of streptocarpus, and very successful they have been. The most important elements of this work are cleanliness, warmth and not overwatering.

Begonias have that kind of leaf that allows them to divide by simply pushing a piece of leaf into some compost. Goodness knows where this has come from, in an evolutionary sense, but it is a pretty handy trick.

Always select perfect leaves for this operation: any browning will result in greater chance of infection. The compost should be free draining, half and half compost and sand very well mixed together is fine.

There are different methods for different plants:

Streptocarpus should be cut along the midrib and then placed in the compost.

Begonia should be cut across the main vein and then put into compost.

Sansevieria should be cut into horizontal strips and placed in compost.

Cover the tray with a propagator lid and lift it off a couple of times a week to air off. The plants also need to be in bright light.

Trees in the garden

Folklore and trees go hand in hand, not only for their longevity and presence throughout our landscape, but also for their health-giving properties. Trees not only allow us to breathe, but they are a wonderfully calming addition to our lives.

Planting a tree in the garden will not only provide you with a focal point for your plot but it will stay with you over the years, becoming an old friend. Maples provide fantastic colour to a garden and can be kept a manageable size, especially if they are planted in a large tub. Hawthorns, too, are a good option for a smaller garden, as they can develop in a similar way to a shrub.

Willow trees need room to spread, though look beautiful mature, as do sweet chestnuts and hazels. Mountain ash will give a lovely display of berries in gardens lacking colour, as will holly, which makes a brilliant hedge.

The best option for smaller gardens is a fruit tree, which will give you food for your table as well as a lovely focal point. Plant a cherry or plum tree in autumn, either in a large container or directly into the ground. Make sure your hole is twice the size of the root ball of your tree, and the deeper the better. Loosen the soil around it and incorporate some fertilizer before you start. Ensure the soil around the tree is compacted down to make sure your tree does not blow over in strong autumnal winds.

CHRISTMAS ROSE

Christmas rose

A lovely addition to the winter garden, blooming whilst most other things are asleep, the Christmas rose, or hellebore, may not flower for the day itself but it will certainly give you a smile through the colder period.

These lovely little plants will reach as tall as 15 inches and have shiny green leaves and white blooms. Hellebores take a while to establish themselves but it really is worth putting in the effort as they will flower at a period when the rest of the garden is doing very little. They like well-drained alkaline soil and will not tolerate dry conditions, though growing them in a pot of compost is helpful as you can move them around as the weather gets bad.

Sow them in pots in early autumn and keep outside, as they need a period of freezing temperatures in order to germinate, then repot them under a cold frame or in a greenhouse in the spring. Keep them in a shady spot and ensure they have a deep pot or hole to live in, as their roots go deep. A layer of mulch around the plant will ensure it does not dry out. As your plants become established, remove dead leaves and feed them with a light liquid feed in the spring.

Gardening notes

Gardening notes

Index